HOWE·LIBRARY

HANOVER
NEW HAMPSHIRE

Also by M. L. ROSENTHAL

POETRY

Blue Boy on Skates
Beyond Power: New Poems
The View from the Peacock's Tail
She: A Sequence of Poems
Poems 1964–1980
As for Love: Poems and Translations

CRITICISM

A Primer of Ezra Pound
The Modern Poets: A Critical Introduction
The New Poets: American and British Poetry Since World War II
Randall Jarrell
Poetry and the Common Life
Sailing into the Unknown: Yeats, Pound, and Eliot
The Modern Poetic Sequence: The Genius of Modern Poetry
(with Sally M. Gall)

EDITIONS

Selected Poems and Three Plays of William Butler Yeats
The William Carlos Williams Reader
The New Modern Poetry: American and British Poetry Since
World War II

The
Poet's
Art

M. L. ROSENTHAL

The Poet's Art

W · W · NORTON & COMPANY

NEW YORK · LONDON

808.1
R81

FOR ACKNOWLEDGMENTS, SEE PAGE 156

Library of Congress Cataloging-in-Publication Data
Rosenthal, M. L. (Macha Louis), 1917–
  The poet's art.
  1. Poetics.   I. title.
PN1042.R57   1987   808.1   86–23535

ISBN 0-393-02432-6

W. W. Norton & Company, Inc., 500 Fifth Avenue, New York, N.Y. 10110
W. W. Norton & Company Ltd., 37 Great Russell Street, London WC1B 3NU

1 2 3 4 5 6 7 8 9 0

For my hostages to love and fortune

Contents

Foreword

The poet's art brings him or her into a realm of exploration. Its object is a recovery, in language, of revelatory awareness in process. Since an artist is at work, the process is to some degree a controlled one. But the control lies mainly in the balancing of the pressures active inside the poem: its structure.

There you have the elements of one theory of poetry, to which must be added that there's nothing abstract or schematic about the process. Each poem has its own idiom, made up of evocative phrases, sounds, silences, rhythms, and tones of every shading. Its character arises within a subjective world of reverie, memory, and traceries of association. Among other things, the history of poetry is the history of that subjective world, in which mankind has dwelt from the start. And it is useful to remember that the history of any art constitutes a living memory antedating not only any one artist but whole eras of the past.

In the present book, meant for readers with a lively interest in poetry, I try to search out my understanding of the art on the basis of my experience as poet and critic. By "experience" I mean direct engagement with the feeling, unfolding, and craft of a great many poems. Such experience, at its best, leads to an intimate empathy with what is going on in a poem. It leads also, and perhaps paradoxically, to the necessary distance from it that gives room for gauging its qualities and problems. Oddly, these two results of attentive experience—empathy and distancing—reinforce one another. This is true for readers but even more so for poets, who must at once let the process of creation take over and yet look upon it with a cold eye. By the acts of writing and revising, one is both making a poem and judging it: giving way to this image or that tone, rejecting others, deciding on a "final" version (or that one hasn't reached it after all).

In my first chapter, "Open Secrets: Poetry as Sheer Good Luck," I focus on the inward candor that nourishes poetry and resists control by objective logic or socially approved stances and inhibitions. As everywhere in this book, my thoughts are related to a number of poems that I quote— poems that have, as it were, offered themselves to me as I considered how the wayward stuff of dream and emotion and sensuous flickerings is captured and converted into poems. Why they should so have offered themselves will be self-evident in some of their titles and first lines: for instance, Dilys Laing's title "Transience of Pain" and the first lines of Verlaine's *"Art Poétique"* (*"De la musique encore et toujours!"*) and of Wordsworth's untitled sonnet beginning "Surprised by joy—impatient as the Wind." Of course, though, it was neither titles nor first lines (however forcefully they thrust themselves forward) so much as the character of poems themselves that made them seem fruitful instances. I quote from some nine poems in the first chapter (and from an average of about as many more in the others), but in doing so have felt like Odysseus fighting off the throng of eager shades near the entrance to Erebus. Most poems of any quality could have served as examples for any of the chapters, but some presented themselves more vividly than others in their particular contexts.

The second chapter, "Growing into Poetry," has to do with how poetically gifted persons mature into artists and how, in a parallel process, the most responsive readers develop. It deals, too, with the way an individual poem evolves from whatever set it going in the first place. We all have the volatile awareness found in poetry (the subject of my book *Poetry and the Common Life*). It is left to the poet, however, to detect its presence and find the language and form to bring it to the surface. The sensitized reader, if not a poet, has at least grown into sympathetic receptivity to this process.

Chapter Three, " 'Perilous Aspect': The Dark Side of the Art," dwells on the depth of serious engagement with humanity's most drastic concerns that can be found in poetry. Even poems that begin lightly and whimsically may take a disturbing turn not originally envisioned by the poet. In its most destructive form, the movement is into realizations that are death-haunted or tragically premonitory, or that undercut cherished illusions inseparable from personal self-regard. The discussion is extended in Chapter Four, "The Clear, Elusive Poem-in-Itself," where major attention goes to the dynamics of poetic structure in work of extreme seriousness (as opposed to discursive argument and polemical rhetoric). I have therefore reserved for this fourth chapter a set of key terms and definitions useful to the analysis of the lyrical structure, or dynamics, of poems. The application of these concepts will, I hope, have been thoroughly illustrated by this point in the book, so that it will be clear that they are derived from specific poems and their observable qualities. They are useful as aids toward seeing into the life of a poem, not as a priori principles to be imposed on poems or substituted for them.

The title of Chapter Five, "Form: The Poem's Musical Body," is doubtless self-explanatory. I am not concerned here with laying out general principles of prosody and other aspects of verse-technique, although I certainly draw upon them constantly. The emphasis, rather, falls on their qualitative function in poems: their active reinforcement of the dynamics in light of the approach developed in the preceding chapters. They are not "merely" mechanical elements to be learned by rote but vital and formative in their own right. In this context, it has seemed relevant also to consider the art of translation and to introduce the subject of prose-poetry.

The final chapter, " 'Rigor of Beauty': Poetic Evaluation," brings all that has gone before to bear on the complex questions of what "great" poetry is and what evaluation entails. The expressive (rather than discursive) character of poetry becomes sharply decisive here; so does the way poets of genius pick up from one another and yet blaze their new, independent trails. In great poetry the leap of vision beyond the apparent limits of an author's experience, sometimes forcing totally unexpected reversals, requires the resurrection of once honored words like "transport" and "magic," freed of sentimental and facile abuse. Evaluation does not reach for absolute judgments, however, but is a process of weighing what's there—of empathy and repossession—whether engaged with famous works or largely unknown ones.

A quick glance through the index will show the poems (and certain prose and dramatic works) against which my thoughts can most readily be tested, although mostly they "tease us out of thought." I've had great instructors—Dante, Shakespeare, Whitman, Rilke, Joyce, and the rest—and they stand willing to show to all and sundry just what part of the world's business goes on within us, amazingly, day after day.

Suffern, New York
July 1986

De la musique encore et toujours!
Que ton vers soit la chose envolée
Qu'on sent qui fuit d'une âme en allée
Vers d'autres cieux à d'autres amours.

Que ton vers soit la bonne aventure
Éparse au vent crispé du matin
Qui va fleurant la menthe et le thym . . .
Et tout le reste est littérature

— PAUL VERLAINE

ONE

Open Secrets:
Poetry as Sheer
Good Luck

Is there a place where grown men and women can be perfectly honest, naïve if need be, without reproach or fear or ridicule? Where we can probe for, and speak out, whatever is in our hearts, in whatever mood? Where we need never hide a glancing thought from ourselves or others but can net it in its spectral mental haunt, fetch it out into the open, and linger with it there for the pleasure of having it? Or, if its meaning goes another way, face it in all its grossness, or horror, or sheer wretchedness, or humiliation?

No, I suppose not. Not even in our minds' unselfconscious reveries where anything goes—until we notice just what it is that's going and either repress or lose it (if it hasn't already slipped away without ever being noticed at all).

Except, that is, in art—especially in poetry, the art that uses language to delight the heart or break it but also to open it to itself. In the lines from his *"Art Poétique"* quoted in the epigraph, Paul Verlaine admonishes himself (my rough translation):

> Music again and always!
> Let your verse be a winged living thing
> Fleeing, we feel, from a soul in flight
> Towards other skies, to other loves.
>
> Let your verse be sheer good luck
> Scattered in the crisp gusts of morning wind
> That arrive breathing mint and thyme . . .
> And all the rest is just literature.

The other arts strike as deep and as subtly, no question of it; and if I pushed hard enough into the matter I might, indeed, all too easily find myself arguing myself down. Still, the art that uses language lives the most dangerously, for words hit the logical faculty almost as soon, and almost as strongly, as they do poetry's primary targets, the ear and the heart—and logical implications can distract us grievously from the poem's evocative movement. There is a uniquely continuous pressure of expression in a poem that has little to do with rational proof. It commits the poet to reaching for the revelatory "right" language lurking in a nestful of perception, memory, and association. The search is for the essence of the doubly elusive "winged living thing" in phrasing that will seem but a breath of sound yet evoke our inmost sense of reality.

"Music again and always!"—whatever else may be involved. It is the music of poetry that frees up its associations, turning apparent riddles into models of clarity, as in T. S. Eliot's "Burnt Norton":

Garlic and sapphires in the mud
Clot the bedded axle-tree.
The trilling wire in the blood
Sings below inveterate scars
Appeasing long forgotten wars.
The dance along the artery
The circulation of the lymph
Are figured in the drift of stars
Ascend to summer in the tree
We move above the moving tree
In light upon the figured leaf
And hear upon the sodden floor
Below, the boarhound and the boar
Pursue their pattern as before
But reconciled among the stars.

Here the poem has created its own space of freedom, within which to follow through its strangely sensuous insight, however foreign to "normal" speech. As the passage moves, conventional syntax dissolves into a syntax blurred by reverie. A self-induced mystical entrancement, bolstered by hypnotic sound-echoings, dominates the process. The passage begins with two complete sentences, but thereafter the grammatical units, like the images, collapse into one another, with no period until the very end and only one bit of internal punctuation (absolutely necessary to prevent syntactic disaster, but masterful in doing so with minimal fuss). The form is an intricate pattern of repetitions, irregularly occurring but frequent rhymes, and parallel phrasings, all contained within the densely concrete four-stress lines. It provides a rich lingering within the powerful but unstable vision of imagined ascent.

We may read many things into the passage, such as the assumption of an infinitely varied yet consistent rhythmic design throughout the universe, mirrored in the very form of the poem. We may detect something like a distanced personal complaint, a trapped sense of being mired in our muddy, clotted earth and a related predicament of being compounded of filth and exaltation. The passage seems to speak of "scars" from repressed internal struggles as well as from humanity's "forgotten wars" of historical and spiritual development. And the echoes of earlier poets (Mallarmé, Shakespeare, Chapman, Dryden, Milton) show how their sensibilities have extended Eliot's—for art is never purely personal in its origins or execution.

Such observations, though not central, reflect notes of true if specialized interest that are floating realities of the poem and that add to its atmosphere of inspired intelligence. Yet they would count for nothing were it not for the lines' combined nervous intensity and passionate transport as they act out their progression from bafflement, loss, and tragic memory to a cosmic grandeur and transcendence. The combination is precisely embodied in the vibrato-image, both fey and buoyant, of "the trilling wire in the blood" that "sings" a kind of faith in the ultimate meaning of all we undergo. This key effect is reinforced by the insistent metrical beat, the almost unbroken momentum (virtually no emphatic stops along the way), and the heavy use of monosyllabic rhymes, often identical. "Tree," for instance, is put in end-rhyming position three times, and "stars" twice.

So the passage presses toward exultant affirmation while also embodying something more fatalistic and resistant to such pressure. It flies high *and* is balked, is intimate *and* impersonal—like us!

Thus the *"bonne aventure,"* the good luck of the poem:

to find its balance among conflicting elements, in language that somehow escapes from the "soul in flight." The completion of a poem is the unfolding of a realization, the satisfying of a need to bring to the surface the inner realities of the psyche—whether richly delightful or of a harsher, sand-in-the-teeth variety. Completion is a kind of birth as well, signaled by the detachment of the finished poem from its begetter once it becomes self-contained enough.

The passage from "Burnt Norton" is but one verse-unit in one section of the whole poem, so that it merges with the larger structure. It might well stand by itself, however, as an independent poem and a very pure instance of what we have been talking about. Doubtless the passage has a certain philosophical bearing, and we might be tempted to translate its concentrated, resonant images into abstract ideas as we read along. But that way of reading is death to understanding, for the whole freedom of the poem's special realm lies in the direct impact of the successive images and tones—the mingling of thrilled elation and balked dreariness; of movement "above the moving tree" (and toward the stars) and immersion in the "sodden" cruelty of life below. These gather into a music of necessary contradiction that cannot be reduced to intellectual pronouncements. The poem's life consists of simplicities we apprehend with alerted senses: "the trilling wire in the blood," "the dance along the artery," the "drift of stars."

Contradiction, the balancing of unresolved and often conflicting elements, is so essential to so much poetry of the highest interest as almost to be a principle. The individual phrases have such decisive coloration that they refuse to blend into a defined idea; instead, they become ele-

ments in an elusive state of awareness. Thus, this poem by
Dilys Laing:

TRANSIENCE OF PAIN
(Poem while listening to Rudolf Serkin)

It happens and unhappens
in the recording cortex:
structures of love and
images of suffering
rise and resolve

Wounded fawn in the thicket
I must go to him I must go
Antlers caught in the branches
I cannot bear his terror
I must go to him and I go
but there are no antlers
there is no fawn

Where are we here? Inside a place in the head of someone
in a room who is lost in a train of fantasy and feeling evoked
by the music of a great pianist. The music, it goes without
saying (that is, the poem does not say so explicitly), is
extremely moving, a fact brought out by the wondering
observation in the first line: "It happens and unhappens."
This line is something like the subjective equivalent of a
scientific formulation: an internal recognition of a process
within the emotional life, which the "recording cortex"
reveals in the perspective of recurrence. "Unhappens" is a
marvelous word to suggest that the "structures of love
and / images of suffering" are intrinsic to our natures,
whether or not at a given moment we are literally experi-
encing love or suffering. They are always, to borrow a word
from Susanne K. Langer's ponderings, "virtually" present
in the aesthetically receptive sensibility that makes possible

the conversion of psychological pressures into the forms of art. There, in the space of that sensibility in which the potential and the actual are one and the same, whatever human beings can experience constantly "happens and unhappens." Perhaps, even, it is in this space of sensibility that the crucial emotional evaluations of one's life take place.

The second verse-unit of "Transience of Pain" becomes entirely concrete, as if to remind us that we are most definitely not in the realm of abstract discourse. The generalized "structures of love and / images of suffering" now are replaced by vivid picturings ("wounded fawn in the thicket" and "antlers caught in the branches") and personal emotional outcries of response, followed by a note of virtual action ("and I go") and then the dissolution of the whole pattern in the abrupt closing lines that seem oddly disappointed. The moment of "transient pain" is over, but not the sense of painful needs to be dealt with, needs hidden deep within oneself and also in the world at large. The poem is a disturbance—a reminder, forced by the power and beauty of a musical performance, that the capacity for generous response to pain (wounded fawn, stag trapped by the branches, all victimized innocents) does not in itself solve very much. It is an unresolved disturbance, a state (in this instance musically induced) of panic-tinged arousal— a recognizably familiar yet almost inexpressible condition of awareness.

Take as a comparable example Edward Thomas's "As the team's head brass." The country is England, during World War I:

As the team's head brass flashed out on the turn
The lovers disappeared into the wood.

I sat among the boughs of the fallen elm
That strewed the angle of the fallow, and
Watched the plough narrowing a yellow square
Of charlock. Every time the horses turned
Instead of treading me down, the ploughman leaned
Upon the handles to say or ask a word,
About the weather, next about the war.
Scraping the share he faced towards the wood,
And screwed along the furrow till the brass flashed
Once more.

          The blizzard felled the elm whose crest
I sat in, by a woodpecker's round hole,
The ploughman said. "When will they take it away?"
"When the war's over." So the talk began—
One minute and an interval of ten,
A minute more and the same interval.
"Have you been out?" "No." "And don't want to, perhaps?"
"If I could only come back again, I should.
I could spare an arm. I shouldn't want to lose
A leg. If I should lose my head, why, so,
I should want nothing more. . . . Have many gone
From here?" "Yes." "Many lost?" "Yes, a good few.
Only two teams work on the farm this year.
One of my mates is dead. The second day
In France they killed him. It was back in March,
The very night of the blizzard, too. Now if
He had stayed here we should have moved the tree."
"And I should not have sat here. Everything
Would have been different. For it would have been
Another world." "Ay, and a better, though
If we could see all all might seem good." Then
The lovers came out of the wood again:
The horses started and for the last time
I watched the clods crumble and topple over
After the ploughshare and the stumbling team.

    This poem is so quietly developed, so homely in its plain
details and apparently desultory dialogue, that one could

hardly credit its volcanic feeling—especially at first reading. The impact is a delayed one. Thomas was already mobilized, in the Artists' Rifles, when he wrote this poem on 27 May 1916. At the time he was a map-reading instructor in England, but he soon applied for a commission in the Royal Artillery and was sent to France the following January. On 9 April 1917 he was killed by a shell in the first hour of the Arras offensive. None of this, of course, can be derived from what the poem gives us: only the sad reality of the war, marked by preoccupation with the chances of being killed or maimed, expressed with a slight veneer of facetiousness too transparent to be anything but grim. We can see how cheerlessly the prospect of going "out" into actual combat is being weighed.

Set against this heavy burden of knowledge and anticipation are the timeless worlds of nature and of "the lovers," who "disappear" into the wood and emerge again later, and the almost timeless world of the ploughman at work. The contrast seems simple, but the natural and human details are loaded with symbols and hints of loss and destruction quite apart from the subject of the two men's conversation: the war—nothing about its supposed noble purpose, but rather the physical risks and the toll of particular lives.

As in Dilys Laing's poem, but far more ruthlessly, there is a relentless march of ominous phrases throughout the poem: "fallen elm," "treading me down," "the blizzard felled the elm," "spare an arm," "lose / A leg," "lose my head," "Have many gone?," "Many lost?," "One of my mates is dead," "they killed him," "night of the blizzard," "the last time," "clods crumble and topple over," "stumbling team." These phrases gather like the accumulation of subtle lighting effects in a theatrical production. Independently of what the surface of the poem (itself gloomy enough) may be presenting, they cling around the casually introduced topic of the war and contrast bitterly with the wistful thought of "another world" and to the almost invisible presence of "the lovers." They make even the flashing brass on the horses' harness appear sinister, like war armor.

In short, they underline the dark fatalism, very close to anomie, with which the war is viewed. The war is something impersonal; ordinary folk haven't a clue to how or why it is happening. At the end, the imagery is full of premonition; a kind of suicidal acquiescence is implicit, a marking-time atmosphere in which terror is held off by understatement, a minimal touch of humor, and the deliberate self-anaesthesis of casual conversation at a ritual pace: "One minute and an interval of ten, / A minute more and the same interval." If there is anger in the situation, it is certainly repressed; yet the frustration and the slaughterhouse prospects do come close to making the dialogue a hysterical exchange instead of the gray, calm thing it purports to be. What unmanly feelings! What revolutionary implications! What longing for the quiet prewar past!

And, at the same time, something far more complex is suggested as well by the supreme irony of the whole poem considered as a masterpiece of implication. The "they" who killed the ploughman's mate in France are, literally, the German enemy. But these are unspecified, and room is left to think of "them" as warmakers generally: that is, all the powers responsible for all the killing. That responsibility began before the war itself was started—as the poem hardly needs say.

Verlaine's image of the scent of mint and thyme in the fresh morning winds is not quite apt for the music and spirit of a poem like Thomas's. Still, the main point of *"Art Poétique"* is that true poetry breathes its felt awareness, rather than spelling out positions rhetorically. The most famous line in the poem advises: *"Prends l'éloquence et tords-lui son cou!"* ("Take eloquence and wring its neck!") Eloquence— rhetoric in its most obvious sense—is just what Thomas avoids at all costs, even at the risk of burying his real attitudes so deep that his language no longer fully implies them. A purer eloquence resides in poetry that runs this risk.

Realistically speaking, we cannot begin to grasp our inner sense of existence unless we bring the buried life of reverie, feeling, and dream into the foreground of consciousness and, somehow, connect it with the surface events of daily experience. This latter connection is especially elusive. After all, a country walk and a conversation such as Thomas describes would seem experiences too obvious to need probing for what they "really mean"—unlike a mood or a dream or a startling image in the mind's eye. The clue will lie in the plastic use of language—that is, the phrasing and tone and rhythms by which the experiences are conveyed—just as with the conveying of the buried life. If we ask precisely what it is a poem does, the answer has much to do with this indispensable function, at once humanly immediate and artistically distanced. It is curious that the accuracy and discipline needed to reveal an exact state of subjective awareness should depend on something like irresponsibility: "mere" pleasure in language and sound for their own sake; openness to the freest play of association, to the point of apparent frivolousness; and a receptivity to the realities of empirical experience, the visions of fantasy, and modes of belief and self-gratification not one's own that amounts to amorality—

> Let your verse be a winged living thing
> Fleeing, we feel, from a soul in flight
> Towards other skies, to other loves.
>
> Let your verse be sheer good luck . . .

For art shows us, not what is right or wrong, but how it feels to be alive—what goes on in us whether or not we like it and, for that matter, whether or not the artist likes it. Obviously, art works as an extension of the nervous system, interacting with whatever impinges on it; and artistic sensibility (that is, the whole capacity for subjective awareness) responds to more than physical stimuli. It responds to everything that might affect human beings: psychological pressures generally, whether of a moral or emotional or social character. (And most psychological pressure involves sensuous elements as well as these others.) The primary response is not judgmental but a kind of imprinting of the way the impact feels. Thus, Verlaine records the spirit with which genuine poetry comes into being, and Laing the troubling pictures induced in the mind by music she is hearing, and Thomas a condition of desolate entrapment and the posing of a desperate choice. The "sheer good luck" is for the poet the good luck of discovering a center of feeling and its context, and the discovery may or may not be a happy one. The whole morality lies in truthfulness to the feeling or perception, and in following through to wherever the implications may lead.

To pick up Eliot's image, "the trilling wire in the blood" connects the private and the universal and provides pitch and melody for the poet's song. Something like childish questioning and wonder, and the sudden appearance of what another poet (Wallace Stevens, in "Thirteen Ways of

Looking at a Blackbird") called a mood that "traced an indecipherable cause," are certainly involved. But it is a more adult persistence, the energy of aroused intelligence and passion to get the whole of a set of feeling in view, that makes the delight of poetry also a dangerous pursuit.

To be alive on this island in space—the earth, but also the island of humanity's sense of itself in a universe made up of impersonal fields of process—is like the "sheer good luck" of a poem. To have life, and to be able to see that we have it and to savor it consciously and contemplate it, is in itself a joy. But then, the condition has its components of misery and ghastly horror "upon the sodden floor" where "the boarhound and the boar" forever "pursue their pattern" of life-and-death struggle, and where we are never free of the knowledge of terror "I cannot bear," and where men must pretend to joke about whether they would find it most convenient, in the course of a war, to lose an arm, a leg, or a head. But even without the interference to joy of every kind of savage injustice (exploitation, helpless suffering, and officially sanctioned mass-murder do not exhaust the list), there is a variety of bleak zestlessness endemic to certain personalities that actually gives them pleasure and can lead to poetry. Philip Larkin is a prime example:

High Windows

When I see a couple of kids
And guess he's fucking her and she's
Taking pills or wearing a diaphragm,
I know this is paradise

Everyone old has dreamed of all their lives—
Bonds and gestures pushed to one side

Like an outdated combine harvester,
And everyone young going down the long slide

To happiness, endlessly. I wonder if
Anyone looked at me, forty years back,
And thought, *That'll be the life;*
No God any more, or sweating in the dark

About hell and that, or having to hide
What you think of the priest. He
And his lot will all go down the long slide
Like free bloody birds. And immediately

Rather than words comes the thought of high
            windows:
The sun-comprehending glass,
And beyond it, the deep blue air, that shows
Nothing, and is nowhere, and is endless.

The double movement of this poem is peculiar. Look
at the surface effects alone and you will be struck by the
deliberate grossness and almost malicious irony of the first
stanza and the contrasting purity of expression and paradoxical melancholy of the closing stanza. In between, the
three middle stanzas, still ironic but more serious than the
first in tone, expand on the illusion of a blissful freedom
denied to oneself that successive generations feel looking
at their juniors. Just as the speaker sees "paradise" in the
sloughing-off of sexual inhibitions by the young, so his
elders saw it in the abandonment of religion by his generation. These middle stanzas make a slightly bitter verbal
bridge to the exalted, lyrically entranced sadness of the
ending. At the same time, the final image, evocative of
church windows while not at all explicitly specifying them,
focuses a vision of dazzling, disappointing illusion that

equates eternity with nothingness. The closing stanza both ennobles and mocks the lesser illusions presented earlier on, of bliss through sexual freedom, bliss through freedom from religious guilt, and, by implication, bliss of any sort.

Larkin is on shaky ground. We may (I do) dismiss the too-easy denigration of the mind's progress toward freedom that dominates his thinking. Sexual liberation is not promiscuity or reducible to "he's fucking her" but involves a shift in sensibility undreamt of in this poem; and freedom from conventionally religious mentality is hardly freedom from conscience or responsibility. Nevertheless, "the deep blue air, that shows, / Nothing, and is nowhere, and is endless" is another matter altogether. Taken as sympathetically as possible, the closing stanza redeems the partial paltriness of what precedes it. It provides a strange balance, for it can hardly satisfy the human dream of a truly rich freedom although its phrasing presents the dream in appropriate terms. The phrase "high windows," especially, echoes the title in standing out against the stanza's ultimate mood, telegraphed in the petty spirit of the poem's beginning.

Another dimension of the poem lies in the simple fact that its different levels of sensibility do reflect the way reverie takes place. The blunt physicality of the opening observation, however vulgar the observer's mentality at the moment the thought intrudes itself, could indeed pass through anyone's mind for reasons having to do with the circumstances of observation or just some quirk or nudge of impulse. The source of the impulse may simply be the new fashions of colloquial speech, probably combined with the half wry, half self-burlesquing feeling of deprivation merely because one has been born in the wrong generation—a feeling Larkin has also expressed elsewhere, in his wittier, bouncier, shallower "Annus Mirabilis":

> Sexual intercourse began
> In nineteen sixty-three
> (Which was rather late for me)—
> Between the end of the *Chatterley* ban
> And the Beatles' first LP.

To return to "High Windows," the supposed widely shared comic chagrin of an older generation at the fun it has missed starts things off in rather aggressive style. Then, as if the poem sought to get out from under its embarrassment at giving the game away, a counterpressure to indulging in such chagrin makes itself felt. The phrase "down the long slide / To happiness" sounds more doomladen than liberated in tone; and the negation gains force in the italicized lines, whose vehemence outweighs their wistfulness. The closing stanza abruptly cuts off this buildup of difficult, resentful emotions with its chilled sense of empty existence.

The result is a balancing, and then a quick freeze, of unpleasant and unruly emotions in a highly depressive context. The complex tonal oppositions here could hardly be conveyed with such compressed impact otherwise than in a poem. From the first quick pang of contemptuous (and perhaps self-despising) physical envy to the poised imagery of cold despair at the end, the poem's curve of life-denial works itself through dynamically. The series of quatrains provides a surface regularity of form; but the movement is actually made up of a succession of wrenching shifts of perspective, subliminally marked by the changing patterns of rhyme and line length and the varied levels of formality in the diction. The sense of frustration, the uneasy nastiness, and the vision of the sublime as pure mockery are fused into a piteously hostile and thwarted state of sensibility, nervously witty and trapped within itself.

Joy, felt to be enviable but ultimately impossible, and depression, seen as life's basic condition, are placed in corrosive opposition in Larkin's poem. The same opposition has a very different quality in poetry less fearful of emotional commitment (although fear of emotional commitment *is* perhaps, however paradoxically, the dominant emotion in much of Larkin's work, felt with all intensity and genuineness in "High Windows"). The first line alone of Wordsworth's sonnet "Surprised by joy—impatient as the Wind" reveals a soul in a different realm entirely, so overwhelmed by feeling and desirous of sharing it that the struggle it suffers through has no touch whatsoever of wary self-consciousness:

> Surprised by joy—impatient as the Wind
> I turned to share the transport—Oh! with whom
> But Thee, deep buried in the silent tomb,
> That spot which no vicissitude can find?
> Love, faithful love, recalled thee to my mind—
> But how could I forget thee? Through what power,
> Even for the least division of an hour,
> Have I been so beguiled as to be blind
> To my most grievous loss?—That thought's return
> Was the worst pang that sorrow ever bore,
> Save one, one only, when I stood forlorn,

Knowing my heart's best treasure was no more;
That neither present time, nor years unborn
Could to my sight that heavenly face restore.

What "joy"? what "transport"? The poem does not tell:
something rather strange for Wordsworth, who ordinarily
presents a scene or situation in some very evocative detail.
An emotional state, then, arrives here without warning from
somewhere within oneself. It is a state that could, must,
but cannot be shared with one person only—and that person, as is recalled with a rude shock as sudden as the first
feeling, is no longer alive. So the glorious moment reported
in the first line, almost as though it came on the "crisp
gusts of morning wind" from "a soul in flight" that Verlaine's images present as the carriers and scatterers of true
poetry, turns into its opposite. It projects as bitter, and
permanent, a state of irretrievably grieved frustration as
the one we found in Larkin's final stanza—but more bewil-
dered. There is neither irony nor satire nor distrust of one's
own emotions in the sonnet. Instead, there is dismay at the
betrayal of the very "love, faithful love" that "recalled thee
to my mind" in such a way as to show that, for the moment,
"I [had] been so beguiled as to be blind / To my most
grievous loss." Self-reproach becomes part of the keen
reminder of the loss itself in the long middle section of the
poem, but then is replaced by the recollection that the "worst
pang" was the fact of the death itself and the knowledge
that it could never be undone.

The absolute subjectivity of this poem—as it moves ever
more deeply into the pain of remembered loss and irrevocable if momentarily suppressed grief ("for the least
division of an hour")—does not prevent it from being daz-

zlingly clear. This is so despite the fact that no person is named in the poem, which one would ordinarily think must be addressed to a loved woman now dead. Wordsworth, however, attached an odd note to the poem: "This was in fact suggested by my daughter Catharine long after her death." Catharine had died in 1812 at the age of three. Although Wordsworth had written a poem ("Characteristics of a Child Three Years Old") while she was still alive that delighted in her charming nature, it was a father's poem of pleasure in a baby girl's innocent mischief: "Loving she is, and tractable, though wild," a "happy Creature" with a "pretty round / Of trespasses." It hardly seems likely he would have turned to her to tell about a moment of joyous transport that came mysteriously from nowhere. One can only think that the note was deliberately or unconsciously diversionary, while recognizing the difficulty of identifying the person—if a real person—the poem addresses. Conceivably she is Wordsworth's sister Dorothy, with whom he had been so close before his marriage, but then the "death" would be a symbolic rather than a literal one. Or perhaps another symbolic death, the final breaking-off with Annette Vallon, mother of their illegitimate daughter Caroline, is being referred to. It is even possible, despite the phrases "faithful love" and "heavenly face," that the reference is not to the death, real or symbolic, of a woman but to Wordsworth's temporary estrangement from Coleridge (which ended, however, shortly after the child's death). Whatever the biographical facts, the poem—as all poems must—has converted them into the projection of an internal state that may be the distillation of many intricately related psychological pressures.

Here again, the act of making the poem has allowed revelation that would seem at once ambiguous and too self-exposing in ordinary conversation. This is directly due to the fact that poetic form, in the hands of a writer who understands that he or she is making a work of art and not a versified anecdote or diary entry, by its very nature compels the distancing of poem from poet. The emotional resonances of language are the primary resources of the poet's art. Wordsworth mobilizes them in the form of a Petrarchan sonnet with a decisive, tragically darkened turn in line nine, at the start of the sestet. In that line we find both an abrupt shift to strong personal statement and the jolting conclusion of the poem's series of questions. There are comparably jolting effects elsewhere, whenever we find two or more stresses bunched together so as to interrupt the smoother iambic flow. (See the third, fifth, and eleventh lines especially.) The more the formal structure disciplines the structure of feeling created by sounds, pauses, and phrasing, the greater the concentration of emotional power that gathers and is contained within the poem—and the more truthful and suggestive of internal states the poem becomes.

No accumulation of external biographical details, and no abstract characterization of the abyss of bereftness the poem drops into after its exuberant start, could provide the intimate particularity of feeling the poem unfolds. That feeling could only be driven further underground by detailed autobiographical information, even in the hands of a talented confessional poet like Robert Lowell. In Lowell's work there is often a problem sorting out the genuine poetic music and revelation from the exhibitionistic packing that encases them—although, since no material is absolutely forbidden to poetry, it is only fair to note that even the crassest self-exposure may find its proper music in a true poem. It is not the "facts" given us in a poem but the quality and physical resonance and rhythm of the phrasing that connect in such a case. Thus, the ending of Lowell's famous poem "Skunk Hour":

> One dark night,
> my Tudor Ford climbed the hill's skull;
> I watched for love-cars. Lights turned down,
> they lay together, hull to hull,
> where the graveyard shelves on the town. . . .
> My mind's not right.
>
> A car radio bleats,
> "Love, O careless Love. . . ." I hear
> my ill-spirit sob in each blood cell,
> as if my hand were at its throat. . . .
> I myself am hell;
> nobody's here—
>
> only skunks, that search
> in the moonlight for a bite to eat.
> They march on their soles up Main Street:
> white stripes, moonstruck eyes' red fire
> under the chalk-dry and spar spire
> of the Trinitarian Church.
>
> I stand on top
> of our back steps and breathe the rich air—
> a mother skunk with her column of kittens swills
>   the garbage pail.
> She jabs her wedge-head in a cup
> of sour cream, drops her ostrich tail,
> and will not scare.

Lowell tells us more about himself here than he needs to, but a sufficient infusion of wry satire and a brilliant shift of focus at the end—from himself to the skunks marching doughtily through village streets to forage in garbage cans—take the curse off an all-too-ready self-pitying claim to distinguished degradation. There is a vast difference, within the four stanzas that end the poem, between the maudlin first pair and the simultaneously intense and humorously distanced closing pair.

Dauntless, eerie, demonic with their "moonstruck eyes' red fire," these nocturnal and odoriferous mammals also have their dignity and charm. In the decaying village, with its sterile religious edifice, they move triumphantly and unabashedly towards what they want. For the demoralized speaker, they are an object lesson in self-acceptance and gratification without guilt. The passage as a whole, though, presents effects at once psychically disturbed and aggressive; despite the "positive" side of the skunks, it suggests a possibly perverse or infantile ideal of mental health. A restlessly varied scheme of rhyme-placement and line-length contributes to the impression of disorder, as if the poem itself sought a regular form but was too perturbed to sustain one. Meanwhile, lyrical snatches like the song-refrain "Love, O careless Love" help provide an atmosphere of embittered yearning. Also, there are subtle echoes of other poems that belie the speaker's apparent lowliness of spirit. In line 11, for example, the outcry "I myself am hell" comes directly from the proud, heroically desolate words of Satan in Milton's *Paradise Lost;* and in lines 19–20, the phrasing recalls—distantly but distinctly—the romantic stance of Yeats's line "I pace upon the battlements and stare" in "The Tower." Such associations can approach the subliminal and will not be obvious to all readers. Still, they are present and contribute to the way a "secret" identification with the skunks contradicts the poem's apparent pathos and creates a counterpointing music of amoral insistence.

Offhand, one would think Lowell's poem light-years away in spirit from a robustly erotic poem like "To His Mistress Going to Bed," by Shakespeare's contemporary, John Donne. Donne's poem has its sophisticated aspects, philosophical and perhaps even theological. But its dominant tone is lustily joyous, as in these lines:

> License my roving hands, and let them go
> Before, behind, between, above, below.
> O my America! my new-found-land,
> My kingdom, safeliest when with one man
>   manned,
> My mine of precious stones, my empery,
> How blest am I in this discovering thee!
> To enter in these bonds, is to be free;
> Then where my hand is set, my seal shall be.

The combined licentiousness, bliss, courtly adoration, and even political exuberance (for the language breathes of Elizabethan glories of conquest and exploration as well as of lovers' intimacies) is a triumph of free expression. The frank language is redeemed from mere sensual wallowing by its happy, witty bawdiness and brilliant play of thought, and by the sense conveyed that the whole feeling is shared by the woman, who is being addressed with a fully admiring and companionable gallantry. This sense of a shared life of body and mind together, of the sort that lovers feel is peculiarly, and exclusively, their own, arises from the poem with a vigorous rapture that makes ordinary modesty and moral restraint seem irrelevant. The succession of rhyming couplets, each an ingenious, self-contained outcry of unreserved delight, builds up to a powerful accumulation of feeling, at once uninhibited, amoral, and sparklingly intelligent and warmly alive. The only similarity to the Lowell passage lies in the implied idealizing of untrammeled physical gratification. In Donne's poem the feeling is masked by wit, elegance, and imagination; in Lowell's, by the notes of abject self-deprecation.

Poetry's freedom can be literally terrifying to readers, or else may challenge approved attitudes too suddenly or severely to be grasped easily at face value. And yet, because anything a man or woman can feel nourishes our understanding, it is a privilege when we are exposed to even the most drastically revealing state of awareness. Pure, unalloyed happiness might be preferable but, if attainable only by blotting out the darker side of experience, would soon prove mere shallowness. The sheer good luck of poetry has its risks, like the luck of being born.

TWO

Growing into Poetry

*T*he *"good luck"* of a poem's birth starts in a certain place
in the mind: the realm of subjective reality where we pass
all hours, waking or sleeping, and where art and reverie
meet. Poets often speak of it, with a special grave absorption. Ezra Pound, imprisoned after World War II on charges
of treason, consoled himself by writing (in Canto 76):

> nothing matters but the quality
> of the affection—
> in the end—that has carved the trace in the mind
> dove sta memoria.

"The quality of the affection" has to do, precisely, with
the depth and richness of what goes on in that inner realm
where memory lingers ("dove sta memoria") and feeling
prevails. Similarly, William Butler Yeats, in "The Tower,"
confronts old age with all his resources—the sum of his
memories of love and friendship, of incisive intellectual
and artistic experience, and of the play of imagination:

I have prepared my peace
With learned Italian things
And the proud stones of Greece,
Poet's imaginings
And memories of love,
Memories of the words of women,
All those things whereof
Man makes a superhuman
Mirror-resembling dream.

These two passages are models of superb poetry that happen also to open onto their authors' compelling motivations. I cite them to introduce the subject of the almost invisible process whereby we, either as writers or as readers, grow into poetry. Though not at all neatly definable, stages of such growth do exist. They have to do with an elusive progress away from purely private utterance toward an impersonal transcendence that is still charged with emotion.

The quoted passages are perfect examples—the work of men in their sixties with unusual creative energy, concentrating a lifetime's accumulated insight into their phrasing. The assertions are positive but not facile. Grief and bitterness, the hardships of the human way, have been absorbed into them; they are ponderings laden with ripe self-knowledge that nevertheless have no egocentric digressiveness. It would certainly be good if the usual level of human exchange were of this order! The *thoughts* in themselves are not abstruse, not difficult, but the set, the tone, of the language invites contemplation and unsentimental sympathy rather than either debate or ready assent. Pound's lines are a tiny unit but could withstand much analysis. They make for a subtle balancing of sounds and rhythm, a quiet implosion of realization made up of varied falling rhythms between the initially resigned "nothing matters" and the beautiful closing claim that memory does matter.[1] The Yeats passage, with its three-stress lines and alternating rhymes, has a gaudier surface while presenting an equally subtle state of adjustment to incompletely accepted defeat.

How poets develop such combined immediacy and mastery is a puzzler, and how people become responsive readers for whom poetry is an essential aspect of their sense of life is another. I am sure that the capacity for both kinds of growth is innate in all people, a necessary aspect of the indispensable gift of language. But we know the obstacles. It is a rare, fortunate child who grows up with books and has heard much reading aloud, and who has lived among adults—if only parents and teachers—used to expressing and discussing ideas and to quoting from poems that breathe the mint and thyme of their true concerns. And even so, there may well be psychological barriers leading a child to reject or ignore such an influence. Moreover, poets and their readers do not become what they are simply by virtue of culturally privileged upbringing. Among the poets of my own acquaintance, few have such a background; a fair number are the first real *readers* as well as the first writers in their families. The old saying that poets are born, not made, probably has something to it. But mainly it is a matter of some quickening though very possibly fortuitous influence: a psychological awakening, not unlike that which informs the making of individual poems, to the omnipresence—in language and in ourselves—of the poetic principle.

[1] The Italian phrase *"dove sta memoria"* is from Guido Cavalcanti's *"Donna mi prega,"* much loved and twice translated by Pound.

Whoever has been so quickened will grasp this omni-presence in a thousand ways. If we return for a moment to one line of Yeats's—"Memories of the words of women"—it will be apparent that there is nothing very sensational about this line. Other phrases in the passage I have quoted, such as "the proud stones of Greece" and "a superhuman / Mirror-resembling dream," call greater attention to themselves. They have, respectively, an eloquently aristo-cratic glamour and a trancelike grandeur. On the surface, both phrases stand in contradiction to the passively pious tone of the opening line, "I have prepared my peace," which suggests the tranquility of an anchorite or a dying saint. "Memories of the words of women," almost offhand in its simplicity, nevertheless draws us more deeply into the world of reverie than any of these other effects. The atmosphere of lovers' conversation, and of distancing from love, per-haps, and of unstated revelations of female sensibility hav-ing nothing to do with matters of love is a complex mixture indeed to be evoked by so unpretentious-sounding a line. The range of tones and intensities of the passage as a whole is enormous, but this one line of almost ordinary discourse brings them all into focus. It recalls what has mattered most and grounds the grander phrases of the passage in the unresolved psychic realities (recognizable to all, yet still strange and even exotic) of love-memory. Precious gains, irrevocable loss, and irreversible knowledge that is colored by desire and yet detached from it are all implied in this quite plain and gently floating line.

Almost any phrase one could think of might, in the right context, serve such a function. Apart from the fact that the sound of human speech is in itself full of music—pings and dings and growls and grace notes and crackling firework explosions—it is studded with touches of poetic originality. We are constantly nudged toward glee or sadness, fear or anticipation, by the harsh or mellow or ironic language of the streets and of factory, bedroom, kitchen, or office. The style of a popular comedian or a more serious actor or actress; a politician's feeling for folk idiom or gift of elegant rhetoric; the catchy malapropisms of a well-liked baseball manager; the pathetic outcry of a stolen child's mother, heard on television—of such elements, as well as the more intimate sounds and phrases of the private life from babyhood onward, is the stuff of poetry made. Poets are thrice-born at least: first, when they discover in themselves a love of the sounds of language and a desire to make attractive shapes with them; next, when they come alive to the riches of the speech around them; and third when they realize they have let themselves in for practicing an art and not merely recording what they hear or "expressing themselves." (Not to pretend to be writing Holy Writ, however, I shall qualify this sentence by adding that "rebirth" as a poet comes from every possible source and shift of mood, and many a poet is reborn—or dies—every morning and most evenings.)

The first stage, love of a vital or melodious phrase of whatever emotional timbre, arouses in the nascent poet a feeling of kinship. That is, the outside world, and the language it makes available, connects with our secret inner world even before we are in a position to objectify anything like a separate subjective state of being—a process that can awaken into action at almost any point between early adolescence and middle young manhood or womanhood or even later. (We have many examples of very youthful awakening, from John Keats to Wilfred Owen;

and of "delayed" development, from Walt Whitman to
Ramon Guthrie.) The reciprocal experience, of the awakening of the *non*-poet to poetry, is almost identical with
that of the true poet at first. Witness the large number of
young people who write poems and often seem quite
promising, but who lose the impulse somewhere along the
way as their primary energies go elsewhere. Such people
can later become splendid responders to poetry, having to
some degree got their hands in on the poet's work and
shared a delight in racy or moving speech.

A good many of the most memorable poems—to return
now to the way common speech nourishes poetry—seem
to pick up from colloquial turns that hit the ear convinc-
ingly. One of Donne's poems begins with a shout: "For
Godsake hold your tongue, and let me love." A sonnet by
E. E. Cummings begins with a witty bit of colloquial ruefulness: "goodby Betty, don't remember me." Jonathan Swift
starts off a mock elegy for a hated military man by echoing
the way people often react to news of someone's death:

> His Grace! impossible! what dead!
> Of old age too, and in his bed!
> And could that Mighty Warrior fall?
> And so inglorious, after all!

Each of these poems moves into more formal and serious
tones by the end. In general, poets are unlikely to write
whole poems in a purely colloquial vein. They may keep
the tone fairly informal, but will usually want room to move
through various affective phases. But we do have instances
in which poets have, in fairly short pieces, found sufficient
expression in the unadulterated vernacular. Thus, Langston Hughes's poem "Letter":

Dear Mama,
      Time I pay rent and get my food
and laundry I don't have much left
but here is five dollars for you
to show you I still appreciates you.
My girl-friend send her love and say
she hopes to lay eyes on you sometime in life.
Mama, it has been raining cats and dogs up
here. Well, that is all so I will close.
                    Your son baby
                         Respectably as ever,
                                   Joe

This, like many other poems by Hughes, is virtually a "found poem." It could well have been taken from a real letter and broken into lines, mostly four-stress but hardly regular in pattern. Hughes catches the idiom and grammar of Black English and the essential poverty of the people who speak it in the very grain of his poem. The comic effects in the second half are gentle ones. They would not have been comic by intention if the letter were authentic. But although the poem invites such considerations, we need not pause over them here except to note its ambiguity of feeling and its dependence on external observation and empathy rather than inwardness. Writing the poem demanded considerable skill in balancing humor, tenderness, and realism and in achieving the kind of detachment that allows tones of amusement without condescension, and of understanding without sentimentality, to reinforce one another.

Another poem of Hughes's, "Down and Out," is still more detached. It could easily be a folk or a blues song,

and certainly lends itself to being felt musically because of
its repetitions:

> Baby, if you love me
> Help me when I'm down and out.
> If you love me, baby,
> Help me when I'm down and out,
> I'm a po' gal
> Nobody gives a damn about.
>
> The credit man's done took ma clothes
> And rent time's nearly here.
> I'd like to buy a straightenin' comb,
> An' I need a dime fo' beer.
>
> I need a dime fo' beer.

However, both its abrupt ending and the fact that the
stanzas are not symmetrically parallel make "Down and Out"
a poem shaped out of elements of popular song but
departing from a formal song pattern. Thus it narrows
into a sudden anticlimactic ending, not comic as in "Letter" yet plaintive about the least moving item in the speaker's list of things she desperately needs. Here again, the
poet is nowhere to be seen in the poem despite the total
empathy it reveals.

The artistry of "Down and Out" lies in its rhythmic ear,
subtle imbalance, and fine seriousness free of solemnity.
Not only does it unselfconsciously reflect a way of speech
in a world of miserable squalor, but it also has qualities of
the characteristically plaintive blues songs created by urban
blacks. If its limitation is that it does not go far beyond
what the poet has literally borrowed from these sources (as
"Letter" hardly goes beyond what such a letter would ordinarily contain), it is splendidly accurate and extremely dis-
ciplined in its restraint.

It is interesting to see how another poet, Michael Harper, has taken a long step further in a poem like "Makin' Jump Shots," which combines standard and vernacular expression:

> He waltzes into the lane
> 'cross the free-throw line,
> fakes a drive, pivots,
> floats from the asphalt turf
> in an arc of black light,
> and sinks two into the chains.
>
> One on one he fakes
> down the main, passes
> into the free lane
> and hits the chains.
>
> A sniff in the fallen air—
> he stuffs it through the chains
> riding high:
> "traveling" someone calls—
> and he laughs, stepping
> to a silent beat, gliding
> as he sinks two into the chains.

The boy practicing with a basketball on a city playground (its "turf" is made of asphalt) is presented almost entirely within the frame of his own consciousness. Another person's voice enters that frame for a moment, when someone watching him jokingly calls out the word "traveling," as if he were simply running with the ball—a rule-violation in an actual game—before making his shot. But that voice is in the same world as his own thoughts, which are saturated with the lingo of the game: "the free-throw line," "sinks two," "the chains" (for the basket), "fakes / down the main," "hits," stuffs it." This lingo blends readily with the sparsely distributed colloquialisms " 'cross" and "riding high." (Most of the basketball terms are themselves colloquialisms as well.)

At the same time, the poem reaches beyond the lingo. It is not just accurate impression and local color in phrases like "in an arc of black light" (an image of the player leaping toward the basket, his dark skin glowing) and "stepping / to a silent beat, gliding." A certain symbolic depth, and a sense of the whole scene as an aesthetically reconceived extension of the literal one, are added by this more formal and metaphoric language. As a result, the repetition of the phrase "the chains" at the end of each verse-unit becomes something other than an obvious, shallow, and forced sound-echoing. The subtler connotations of the phrase make themselves felt unobtrusively, so that all the poem's imagery of bold, skillful movement can be experienced both lyrically and ironically. Although the "arc of black light" could not be more alive with power and grace, the expression suggests a limited scope as well. This dimension, of circumscribed control, encompasses the repeated opposites "free" and "chains," as does the concentrated flowing inwardness of the line "to a silent beat, gliding," just before the end. Apart from its physical immediacy, the poem at last projects a state of momentary transport that carries it beyond the unresolved psychic and social pressures it has evoked.

Harper's poem is a clear instance of what William Carlos Williams says in one of his prose-passages in *Spring and All:*

> As birds' wings beat the solid air without which none could fly so words freed by the imagination affirm reality by their flight.

This simile wonderfully focuses the relationship, and the difference, between a poem and the complex matrix that nourished it: the mass of feelings, thought and reverie, and total memory, both private and historically inherited, that its verbal and rhythmic colorations imply. That matrix—call it a sensibility-mass—is in its way tangible. It is the "solid air" of subjective mental reality we all breathe and move through as our natural human element. A poem precipitates out a purely linguistic construct related to a particular state of arousal within that subjective reality. Its words are the "wings" that "beat the solid air," intimately in touch with that element yet also—to the extent that imagination uses words accurately yet in its own way—"free" of it. In poetry at its best, words are chosen for their affective reach even more than for their literal meaning. The reality they evoke is, primarily, a mental reality.

Williams's simile points up the way a poem depends on its matrix but is in no sense identical with it. In so doing, the simile implies the process of growing into poetry as well: that is, of becoming a poet and even, by a sort of mirror- or shadow-reciprocity, of becoming a truly attuned reader of poetry. Most people, immersed in their daily doings, feelings, and relationships, sometimes find ways of expressing themselves fairly clearly and sensitively, although their expression will be largely functional or ceremonial. Often, too, they will take delight in flashing wit or irony, and will admire or cultivate rhetorical prowess. In these senses all are potential poets. But absorption in language carries the poet beyond direct expression.

It carries him or her, first of all, into a realm where a kind of idly facetious word-play often seems to prevail. This superficially frivolous atmosphere actually serves to keep the creative sensibility open and uninhibited; and within it, suddenly, dark and savage or bright and elated verbal energies can at any time emerge. For in this realm images so vividly *seen* as almost to be hallucinations and rhythms charged with emotion but not yet fleshed out with actual phrasing can assert themselves without warning. When they do, they compel a concentration bent on discovering *the* poem that will eventually connect them and realize their bearings.

In trying to push back to the origins of this process, one should recall the passion that wells up in tiny children, often well before they are three, for accumulating and repeating words and their syntactic and rhythmic connections. The sense of language as power comes on in a sudden surge. There is no question that the literal denotation of words is very important to children in this state; but there is no question, either, that something like incantatory ritual is involved even more strongly. Most likely some of this childlike passion and magical sense of language remains compellingly alive in poets and accounts both for their elementary delight in puns and other word-play and sound-play and their feeling that limitless power rides their art if only they can release and channel it in the right ways. It is true that the grownup man or woman who is a poet also has a logical or common-sense side that "knows" all this isn't quite true and says, dispiritedly, with W. H. Auden, that "poetry makes nothing happen"—the darker perspective of a "realism" that poetry by its very nature cannot really believe in. A poem, after all, *is* making things happen through its own action. It is a projection of volatile awareness that must imprint itself on receptive minds and to some degree, for better or worse, reorient them.

A kind of deliberate mystification, not intended to offend (not even to shock bourgeois complacency and hypocritical gentility—the old raffish slogan of *"épater les bourgeois"*) but rather an absorbed engagement with the magnetism of association, attends certain kinds of excellent poetry. It is the source of much hostile response to the learned but often idiosyncratic allusiveness of poets like Pound and Eliot, or to the references to the names of personal acquaintances hardly known to outsiders by Allen Ginsberg and others, or to dramatic scenes or emotional moments presented in ambiguous context. Some of the hostility may be justified: a matter highly dependent on the quality of the poem in question. But it is certainly true that very young poets, often still in their adolescence, take naturally to this somewhat arrogantly "secretive" mode of poetic magic. Talented youngsters of this sort (the phrase is not dismissive, for one must remember that Keats, Rimbaud, Hart Crane, and Lorca must be counted in their number) are not at all disturbed by issues of surface intelligibility when they read other people's poems. Few would be inclined to rush to the library in search of elucidation; they are much more likely to rush to a desk or table and try to write something "like" a poem that has just stirred them, inventing names of people, places, and works as they go along and thus, as it were, seasoning their poems "to taste." A touch of supposed allusion here to suggest philosophical erudition, a dropped name—fictional or not— there to hint at a special coterie possessed of special shared vision, a pseudo-mythical reference gleaned from who knows where or nowhere, *et violà!*—a poem that is a world unto itself.

And indeed, there is something, though hardly *every-*

thing, to be said for simply splashing about in language for the sheer pleasure of it, or even for the sake of happily (or sadly, or both) creating different tonal formations. Not only does it gratify the poet's most egocentric needs—for such writing mainly creates a Rorschach complex of projections of one's own personality. It also appeals especially to readers who are willing to suspend critical discrimination in favor of subordination to other people's clever self-indulgence. And if one thinks, "Poetry is not so much an organic structuring of the heart's language as it is an endless mood-mirroring by verbally acrobatic display," then such self-indulgence may even seem more agreeable than work of richer discipline. When talent and virtuosity are at all visible, some appreciation at least must mingle with the ennui induced by poems going nowhere in particular. They have their attractions even while their art counts for far less than, say, Keats's "Hyperion" fragments or Rimbaud's *"Bateau ivre"*: poems that reveal at least as much power of fantasy but that are driven further, towards realizations of enormous intensity.

A natural and childlike love of language, then, and of inventiveness for its own sake, is surely indispensable for a poet at any stage of development. But ultimately, as "even the weariest river / Winds somewhere safe to sea" (or so we are told in "The Garden of Proserpine" by Swinburne, sweet prince of self-indulgers, whose devotion to "meaning" was as constant as Don Juan's to any one woman), a true poem does arrive at a point of balance or awareness that counts. A poet's highest art is marked by the urge to realization or transcendence beyond even the loveliest pyrotechnics and the wiliest improvisations. Such art naturally employs every variety of bedazzling and seductive technique, but directs it all toward the service of an encompassing structure—thereby, incidentally, rendering it even more dazzling and seductive. Rimbaud's wildly associative metaphoric progression doubles back on itself to floodlight a gentle childhood memory. Keats's "Hyperion" experiments probe the terror of losing, at one and the same time, both power and the identity it depends on; in the process, they embody a historic shift from epic to lyric as the key to poetic discovery of this kind. Keats's characters, figures of vast mythic proportion, find themselves incapable of heroic action. In terms of the traditional epic ideal, they have grown static and impotent. By the same token, though, their subjective awareness—the turmoil of recognizing their transformation, and the literal inward shudder of its enactment[2]—provides a new type of heroic center in poetry.

A modern instance of such realization comes in one of the most engaging and touching passages of Ezra Pound's *Cantos*. The passage (starting "Will I ever see the Giudecca again?"), which occurs in Canto 83, reveals the essential situation of the sequence called *Pisan Cantos*. In it we see the poet during the most difficult days of his life, when he was a prisoner in the United States Army's Disciplinary Training Center (DTC) in Italy at the end of World War II. Charged with treason and struggling to maintain his sanity and self-regard, he coped with his predicament by

---

[2] See "Hyperion: A Fragment," Book I, lines 259–63: "At this, through all his bulk an agony / Crept gradual, from the feet unto the crown, / Like a lithe serpent vast and muscular / Making slow way, with head and neck convuls'd / From over-strained might."

making a poetry of his observations of people and natural
minutiae, his memories, and his fluctuating moods and
associative trains of thought during his imprisonment:

Will I ever see the Giudecca again?
  or the lights against it, Ca' Foscari, Ca' Giustinian
or the Ca', as they say, of Desdemona
or the two towers where are the cypress no more
    or the boats moored off le Zattere
or the north quai of the Sensaria DAKRUŌN ΔΑΚΡΥΩΝ

  and Brother Wasp is building a very neat house
   of four rooms, one shaped like a squat indian bottle
  La vespa, *la* vespa, mud, swallow system
so that dreaming of Bracelonde and of Perugia
and the great fountain in the Piazza
or of old Bulagaio's cat that with a well timed leap
   could turn the lever-shaped door handle
It comes over me that Mr. Walls must be a ten-strike
with the signorinas
and in the warmth after chill sunrise
an infant, green as new grass,
has stuck its head or tip
out of Madame La Vespa's bottle

mint springs up again
   in spite of Jones' rodents
as had the clover by the gorilla cage
  with a four-leaf

When the mind swings by a grass-blade
   an ant's forefoot shall save you
the clover leaf smells and tastes as its flower

  The infant has descended,
   from mud on the tent roof to Tellus,
like to like colour he goes amid grass-blades

greeting them that dwell under XTHONOS   XΘONOΣ
OI XΘONIOI;   to carry our news
        εἰς χθονίους   to them that dwell under the earth,
begotten of air, that shall sing in the bower
        of Kore,   Περσεφόνεια
and have speech with Tiresias, Thebae

    Cristo Re, Dio Sole

in about ½ a day she has made her adobe
(la vespa) the tiny mud-flask

    and that day I wrote no further

There is fatigue deep as the grave.

This small section of Canto 83, its forty lines divided
into nine verse-units of varying form, tone, and complexity,[3] is in itself a masterpiece of virtuosity with many separate points of interacting feeling and suggestiveness. One
tonal stream running through it is the thickly dark one of
depression and hopeless nostalgia established in the first
verse-unit, which dwells on streets and buildings in Venice
and Perugia remembered from happier days and con-
cludes with a Greek word for tears or weeping: ΔAKPYΩN
(transliterated as "DAKRUŌN"). In the fourth verse-unit
("When the mind swings . . .") we have an implied confes-
sion of closeness to hysterical breakdown, held off by concentration on tiny details of nature: the shape of a grass-
blade, the precise reality of "an ant's forefoot," the smell
of a clover leaf. The next-to-last line, "and that day I read
no further," echoes a famous line from the tragic tale of
Paolo and Francesca in Dante's *Inferno,* Canto 5; and the

---

[3] The last line is actually the beginning of a new verse-unit—a transitional note
connecting what has gone before with a new departure of the Canto.

final line in the passage, "There is fatigue deep as the grave," intensifies the atmosphere of heavy despair.

The thirteen-line second verse-unit, however, introduces sprightly and whimsical tones with its description of the building of a wasp's nest, with the male and female personified as Brother Wasp and Madame La Vespa (Italian for "wasp") and their "infant" suddenly poking its "head or tip" out of the nest at the end. Along with the playful (yet accurate) scrutiny of this insect family comes a mildly risqué thought about a fellow inmate, "Mr. Walls," and the memory of a clever cat, adding to the jollier tone flowing through this verse-unit. Although two nostalgic lines—"so that dreaming of Bracelonde[4] and of Perugia / and the great fountain in the Piazza"—hark back to the sadness of the opening verse-unit, this new tonal stream redirects our emotional attention somewhat.

In the next two verse-units that attention shifts, as we have noted, to minute observations (new shoots of mint and clover, grass-blades, "an ant's forefoot") and to the control they help the poet retain over his precarious mental state. These, with whatever reserves of humor he can call on, help stave off being overwhelmed by all the grossly painful pressures. The references to the apparently unpleasant rats kept by one of the DTC officers, and to the "gorilla cage" reserved for highly dangerous prisoners (in which Pound, because of the treason charge, had been held when first brought to the DTC), will suggest the kind of pressures involved.

Thus far, the passage has maintained a shaky balance

---

[4] The meaning of "Bracelonde" is unclear. Possibly the line alludes to Brocéliande, the forest in Arthurian legend in which the magician Merlin was trapped.

between pitiable subjection to these pressures and brave mobilization of everything that might nourish the poet's morale. But in the fifth verse-unit a considerable reorientation takes place. The "infant" wasp re-enters the poem and, for the time being, draws all its attention. This time it is personified as a tiny Odysseus, journeying to parley with Tiresias and others in the realm of death. In the unit Pound fuses whimsy with graver lyrical phrasing at once doom-laden and suggesting heroic destiny: a remarkable encompassment of all the preceding tonalities. In a sense the wasp "infant, green as new grass," has become an imagined reincarnation of Pound himself as well as of Odysseus. Throughout the *Cantos* the adventures of Odysseus have served as a model for the poet's artistic—and psychological, moral, and political—explorations. The baby wasp's descent from his mother's protection to the earth (Tellus, the Roman goddess of earth, or Earth Mother) parodies the poet's symbolic journey as it does that of the hero of Homer's *Odyssey*.

Despite this parody, the poem grows perfectly serious as it approaches the realm of the dead ruled over by Kore— or Persephone, her other name (spelled out in Greek in the eighth line of this unit). Lines four to six repeat the sound of XTHONOS (given in transliteration and then in Greek in line four), meaning "of the earth" or "the underworld," in two further variations: "HOI CHTHONIOI, "those of the underworld"; and *"eis chthonious,"* "to those of the underworld." An underlying preoccupation with death and transfiguration, almost ecstatically elegiac in spirit, thus becomes the dominant emotional perspective of the passage. The Italian prayer that follows ("Cristo Re, Dio Sole": "Christ the King, God of the Sun") seems natural enough after such lyrical evocation of the dead. The little factual unit ("in about ½ a day . . .") that comes next returns us to the world of plain observation just before the two concluding lines remind us of the underlying weary despair.

No better illustration than this passage could be found to show the truth of Williams's observation that "words freed by the imagination affirm reality by their flight." The dramatic situation of the poem (Pound's confinement in the prison camp in Coltano, near Pisa) is biographically and historically real. The insects and flora of the surrounding Tuscan country landscape are also accurately portrayed. And we can clearly see, in these lines, how the element of pure, seductive word-play helps keep the sensibility open so that the deeper subjective realities can come into their own. The first simple instance is the repetition of *Ca'*—the colloquial Venetian form for *Casa* (a named house)—in the second and third lines. This is a nostalgic rather than a facetious play of sound, admittedly. But in the second verse-unit associative whimsy comes fully into its own, and with it the personifying imagination that humanizes the wasp family and prepares us for the powerful, visionary picture of the "infant" as a delicate messenger to the chthonian realm of the dead that will come in the fifth verse-unit. Similarly, the rhythm of nostalgic elegiac questioning, which echoes the ancient *ubi sunt* lyric tradition (best known in various English translations of Villon's refrain *"Ou sont les neiges d'antan"*: "Where are yesterday's snows?"), colors the whole passage with its tone of irreversible melancholy. This tone is immeasurably darkened in the key underworld unit by the language of primitive awe borrowed—as are the rhythmic turns—from Homer. Pound's virtuosity is certainly brilliant in this passage, but it serves to create an atmosphere of noble-spiritedness in the midst of despondency rather than as mere display. (And the reader sensitized to poetry as an art of affective structure can follow the movement readily enough despite surface difficulties of literal meaning.)

A rather strange seventeenth-century poem by Andrew Marvell, "The Picture of Little T.C. in a Prospect of Flowers," presents a related conversion of the language of whimsical charm into an incantation against death and its terrors. The success of this ingenious poem is a special triumph of passionate artistry over incongruous elements:

THE PICTURE OF LITTLE T.C. IN A PROSPECT OF FLOWERS

See with what simplicity
This nymph begins her golden days!
In the green grass she loves to lie,
And there with her fair aspect tames
The wilder flow'rs, and gives them names;
But only with the roses plays,
      And them does tell
What colour best becomes them, and what smell.

Who can foretell for what high cause
This darling of the gods was born!
Yet this is She whose chaster laws
The wanton Love shall one day fear,
And, under her command severe,
See his bow broke and ensigns torn.
      Happy, who can
Appease this virtuous enemy of man!

O then let me in time compound,
And parley with those conquering eyes,
Ere they have tried their force to wound,
Ere, with their glancing wheels, they drive

In triumph over hearts that strive,
And them that yield but more despise.
    Let me be laid,
Where I may see thy glories from some shade.

Meantime, whilst every verdant thing
Itself does at thy beauty charm,
Reform the errors of the spring;
Make that the tulips may have share
Of sweetness, seeing they are fair;
And roses of their thorns disarm;
    But most procure
That violets may a longer age endure.

But, O young beauty of the woods,
Whom nature courts with fruits and flow'rs,
Gather the flow'rs, but spare the buds,
Lest Flora, angry at thy crime,
To kill her infants in their prime,
Do quickly make th' example yours;
    And, ere we see,
Nip in the blossom all our hopes and thee.

Scholars conjecture that "little T.C." was a girl named
Theophila Cornewall, whose older sister had died in childhood. (Infant mortality ran high during the period in any
case, so that the danger was omnipresent in people's minds.)
Marvell's fancy begins to dance around the pretty little
creature at once, so that she is presented as part baby-
goddess and part the object of his pretended courtly love.
That is, the first stanza presents her "taming" the "wilder
flow'rs" by her presence and naming them as though she
were a deity (or Adam naming the animals in Eden) and
instructing the roses in their proper color and fragrance;
and the second and third stanzas adopt the language of
courtly worship of a chaste and disdainful mistress in the

manner of Petrarch and other late-medieval and Renais-
sance poets. The fourth stanza then returns to the notion
of little T.C. as a goddess who can change the laws of nature
itself and "reform the errors of the spring" by giving tulips
a sweet smell, doing away with rose-thorns, and prevent-
ing violets from fading away so soon. This stanza provides
the poem's crucial turn—by way of playful pleading to the
little girl to perform these miracles—to the subject of early
death; the whimsy here has an ironic sting as well, suggesting as it does our helplessness in the face of actual destiny. The suggestion returns with brutal force in the closing
stanza, where the child is urged not to tempt destiny (in
the form of Flora, the true goddess of flowers) to punish
her for plucking young buds by seeing to it that she too
will die early. Playful pretence is sustained throughout the
poem, but each stanza grows more serious than the one
preceding it until at last whimsy is converted to an expression of terror.

It might well be argued that the poem's final grimness
comes on too swiftly despite its brilliant development. On
the other hand, if we read it sympathetically enough,
somewhat discounting an element of "fine sentiment" that
has gone out of fashion, we can see that the garden imagery
is reminiscent in its details of the doomed glory of Eden
and that all the playfulness is delicately tinted with fearful
notes and tender concern throughout the poem's unfolding—and also that the ending has the virtue of taking a
bold risk (like Pound's in his vision of the infant wasp's
Odyssean journey) in coping with a fundamentally intractable dilemma. Marvell has converted the language of
charming tribute into severe realization that encompasses
not only the delights of elegant, mannered speech and
behavior but the knowledge of human vulnerability beneath

all the pretence of custom and the ornamental side of human art. The conversion is beautifully foreshadowed in the touching opening lines concerning the little girl's art-less confidence in the world of nature ("See with what simplicity / This nymph begins her golden days!"); in the second stanza's light irony at the thought that "this vir-tuous enemy of man" will strive to keep men's love at bay some day; in the next stanza's prayer that the speaker will not outlive the child ("Let me be laid, / Where I may see thy glories from some shade"); and in the fourth stanza's ruefulness at the brief life of violets. The intricate rhyme scheme, within a long stanza made up of six four-stress lines followed by a graceful dimeter line (like a courtly dance turn) and then a final five-stress line, parallels the emo-tional structure leading from a lyrical play of attitudes into graver, even tragic feeling.

Readers may find it of some interest to compare a poem by a fashionable contemporary figure, John Ashbery, which he clearly felt to be reciprocal in some way with Marvell's. It is called "The Picture of Little J.A. in a Prospect of Flowers."

THE PICTURE OF LITTLE J.A. IN A PROSPECT OF FLOWERS

He was spoilt from childhood by the future, which he mastered rather early and apparently without effort.

— BORIS PASTERNAK

I

Darkness falls like a wet sponge
And Dick gives Genevieve a swift punch
In the pajamas. "Aroint thee, witch."
Her tongue from previous ecstasy
Releases thoughts like little hats.

"He clap'd me first during the eclipse.
Afterwards I noted his manner
Much altered. But he sending
At that time certain handsome jewels
I durst not seem to take offense."

In a far recess of summer
Monks are playing soccer.

II

So far is goodness a mere memory
Or naming of recent scenes of badness
That even these lives, children,
You may pass through to be blessed,
So fair does each invent his virtue.

And coming from a white world, music
Will sparkle at the lips of many who are
Beloved. Then these, as dirty handmaidens
To some transparent witch, will dream
Of a white hero's subtle wooing,
And time shall force a gift on each.

That beggar to whom you gave no cent
Striped the night with his strange descant.

III

Yet I cannot escape the picture
Of my small self in that bank of flowers:
My head among the blazing phlox
Seemed a pale and gigantic fungus.
I had a hard stare, accepting

Everything, taking nothing,
As though the rolled-up future might stink
As loud as stood the sick moment
The shutter clicked. Though I was wrong,
Still, as the loveliest feelings

Must soon find words, and these, yes,
Displace them, so I am not wrong
In calling this comic version of myself
The true one. For as change is horror,
Virtue is really stubbornness

And only in the light of lost words
Can we imagine our rewards.

The poem presents interesting problems. In Part I, its mixture of riddling, high jinks, and graver effects is intriguing and lively. Despite the title, though, it shows little to warrant the echo of Marvell's title until its third part. There we see that Ashbery is looking at a photograph of himself as a child, taken either in a garden or against a flower-background in a studio. His sullen "hard stare" and "comic" grotesqueness in the picture ("My head among the blazing phlox / Seemed a pale and gigantic fungus") do set his self-image off sharply from Marvell's "young beauty of the woods."

But there any possible implied response to Marvell ends. Ashbery's major tone, even in the awkward, mawkishly written second part, is a sad and bitter one, though less intensely concentrated and earned than Marvell's solicitous fearfulness. But its development is vitiated by the tendency to utter forth easy abstractions like "as change is horror, / Virtue is really stubborness" and "the loveliest feelings / / Must soon find words, and these, yes, / Displace them." The eccentric wit of the poem's opening, together with the bit of disabused and cynical monologue in the first part, holds promise of great liveliness and volatility in the sections to come. Nevertheless, the poem goes dead thereafter until the brooded-over portrait exerts its magnetic pull on the imagination in the opening lines of

Part III—but then the phrasing lapses into abstractions again.

Ashbery's possibilities were clear enough in the more focused parts of the poem, but he avoided following through or at least was unable to direct the progression of his poem with the sure sense of dynamics of a Marvell or a Pound. He has indeed taken us into the inner space of his reveries, memories, and musings, but seems not to have cared (or dared) to try to free his poem from its literal base enough to make it an organic entity in itself. For this reason, incidentally, the epigraph by Pasternak is thoroughly inappropriate. In quoting it, Ashbery seeks to identify himself with its subject, Vladimir Mayakovsky, who at his best was a poet who know how to take great risks and to carry through with all his art. Pasternak's memoir has to do with the work of a revolutionary poet in revolutionary times—his buoyant power, and the way it doomed Mayakovsky to an unwilled political spokesmanship that, once the Russian Revolution had succeeded, went against the grain of his genius. All this, like Marvell's adventurous compression of tender adoration and realistic dread, is a far cry from Ashbery's finally self-entrapped effort.

THREE

"Perilous Aspect": The Dark Side of the Art

*P**leasure, play, wit, comedy:* it is hard, offhand, to think of these words, or concepts, in relation to deeply serious poetry. The connection, in fact, may be the most difficult thing about any art for people to grasp (apart from being attuned to the medium itself if its values—color, bodily movement, spatial balancings, currents of tonality, dynamics, and so on—are unfamiliar). Much of the character of poetry as an art, rather than as mere statement of ideas or personal expression, depends on its quality as formal play. This quality militates against sentimentality (the demand for unearned emotional response) and other sorts of false eloquence. It provides the distancing that allows a poem to build itself as an organic construct in its own right. A classic instance is Ben Jonson's elegy "On My First Son":

Farewell, thou child of my right hand, and joy;
My sin was too much hope of thee, loved boy,
Seven years thou wert lent to me, and I thee pay,
Exacted by thy fate, on the just day.
O, could I lose all father, now. For why
Will man lament the state he should envy?
To have so soon 'scaped world's, and flesh's rage,
And, if no other misery, yet age!
Rest in soft peace, and, asked, say here doth lie
Ben Jonson his best piece of poetry.
For whose sake, henceforth, all his vows be such,
As what he loves may never like too much.

Jonson wrote this poem in 1603, shortly after the boy's death, and one might well wonder how a father could bear to be so clever on such a theme. But the striking and touching fact is that the puns and witticisms are all *serious* ones. There is a hidden pun, for instance, in the first line; the little boy's name was Benjamin, which in Hebrew means "son of my right hand." So the tender phrase "child of my right hand" also names the boy, and the whole opening couplet expresses loving grief. The same thing is true of the climactic pun "Ben Jonson his best piece of poetry," which carries over the double meaning of the Greek word *poetria* (something made or created, and "poetry" in the modern sense) and is also imbedded in a couplet that gently expresses its intense feeling. The final couplet, too, contains a pun—on the word "like," meaning both "love" and "be close kin to"—that enhances the poem's projection of helpless sorrow. Jonson's use of closed couplets is notable here. This form demands a series of sharply pointed effects, since every second line must provide a rhyme that completes its couplet epigrammatically. To be successful, each

couplet must be a whetstone of wit. The combination of
bright verbal play and high formal virtuosity enables the
poem to stay free of easy, obvious emotionalism that would
detract from its precision of feeling.

Jonson's poem, because of both its subject and its technique, naturally reminds one of Marvell's "The Picture of
Little T.C. in a Prospect of Flowers," discussed in the preceding chapter. Marvell's poem, while more complex, is
equally charged with elegant wit that might have been
disastrous for its final balance. But his art proved equal to
the task of controlling the sprightly, courtier-like phrasing
with its whimsical praise of the little girl. The high-spirited
compliments are shot through with terms of dread, among
them "fear," "ensigns torn," "enemy," "crime," and "kill."
The result is far more ominous in tone than a direct
expression of foreboding about a perfectly healthy child
would have been. To sustain a sophisticated play of tone
and style like Marvell's while clearing a path of genuine
emotional realization requires not only sheer skill but artistic morale and courage, the kind seen in a great athlete's
qualities of concentration.

Not to labor the point, but just this sustained pursuit is
missing from John Ashbery's effort, in "The Picture of Little J.A. in a Prospect of Flowers," to achieve something like
Marvell's poem in a twentieth-century way. Ashbery's poem
begins bravely enough, with its opening section toying flip-
ly with interlaced facetious and darker elements, but then
betrays its more vital possibilities. Its larger purpose, I think,
would be to find a valid transition between the initial spir-
ited play of wry tonalities and the drastic insight, centered
in the photograph of the poet as a surly child, at the start
of the final section. The natural procedure, in principle,

would be to follow Marvell's example of surface playfulness, avoidance of easy abstractions, and increasing the pressure (that is, the stress on the horror so gaily masked at first) as the poem develops. Had Ashbery been able to manage this, his early comic free play could have grown into a bitter or sorrowful final impact, kept from sentimentality by an abrasive buffoonery, perhaps, or other harsh effects.

Buffoonery, by the way, is an extremely interesting artistic resource. The emotions it arouses are always mixed, as witness, for instance, the familiar pathos of the clown or the tramp comedian. The deflation of genteel pretensions by the uninhibited stand-up comedian, the suggestion of the ultimate unintelligibility of the universe in so much farce (and in the theatre of the absurd), the humiliations of class, sex, and race or nationality at the root of much popular vaudeville and local-color humor—all these show the clinging web of serious implication that attaches itself to even the most elementary kind of burlesque. To complicate matters further, the comic has obvious dimensions of cruelty as well, and the most sensitive poetry will sometimes exploit an air of brutal indifference to humane feeling to make its mark.

Shakespeare's *Hamlet* has many such passages—interestingly enough, in "prose" for the most part. That is to say, they are in a kind of prose-poetry or pre-modern free verse, with finely balanced rhythmic movement. Thus, the exchange, just before the dumb show in III,ii, between Hamlet and Ophelia, in which he deliberately offends her modesty by his vulgar sexual joking (a reflex of his disgust with his mother's supposed unconscionable wantonness—and hence that of all females, even his beloved Ophelia):

HAMLET Lady, shall I lie in your lap?

OPHELIA No, my lord.

HAMLET I mean, my head upon your lap?

OPHELIA Ay, my lord.   *[He lies at her feet]*

HAMLET Do you think I meant country matters?

OPHELIA I think nothing, my lord.

HAMLET That's a fair thought to lie between maids' legs.

OPHELIA What is, my lord?

HAMLET Nothing.

OPHELIA You are merry, my lord.

HAMLET Who, I?

OPHELIA Ay, my lord.

HAMLET O God, your only jig-maker. What should a man do but be merry, for look you how cheerfully my mother looks, and my father died within's two hours.

[The Queen turns away and whispers with the King and Polonius]

OPHELIA Nay, 'tis twice two months, my lord.

HAMLET So long? nay then let the devil wear black, for I'll have a suit of sables; O heavens, die two months ago, and not forgotten yet? then there's hope a great man's memory may outlive his life half a year, but by'r lady a' must build churches then, or else shall a' suffer not thinking on, with the hobby-horse, whose epitaph is 'For O! for O! the hobby-horse is forgot.'

This sort of buffoonery, in which a noble and highly intelligent young man lets go with a vengeance, serves to amuse in a grotesque way. Chiefly, it expresses emotions too turbulent to control except through conversion into unseemly joking that clearly points to the source of disturbance. The dialogue not only reflects Hamlet's shocked reaction to his mother's behavior but also his anger at the betrayal of his father's memory. His buffoonery intensifies in the closing speech, virtually incomprehensible to a modern audience. The main points made there are that no one is remembered on merit any longer and that one's life is worth no more than a hobby-horse (a comic morris-dance figure in which a man seems to be riding a make-believe horse; or alternatively, a prostitute). In other words, the passage is full of horror and vengefulness, which build up from the jesting harassment of Ophelia in the opening lines to the full-speed, half-ranting attack on the insult to the dead man. (The "epitaph" Hamlet quotes at the end is the refrain of a popular song.)

Dramatically, the Hamlet-Ophelia exchange prepares us for the dumb show, or play within a play, that follows and that explicitly acts out what Hamlet has been referring to: the queen's infidelity and the successful murder of the king. Poetically, it is a floating unit of combined ugly disillusionment and elegiac irony.

Further on in the same scene we have another mocking exchange, this time between Polonius and Hamlet. Again, Hamlet's buffoonery is cruel in intent, although Polonius does not notice how he is being toyed with. The tone of mental bullying would seem despicable, except that the little passage exposes the hypocrisy with which Hamlet is surrounded. Polonius is humoring him because he is the crown prince, but also because he accepts the prince's behavior as evidence of his distracted love for Ophelia. The brief conversation suggests Hamlet's uncompromising mood; despite its evanescent character, it foreshadows the drastic incidents that follow and that result in Polonius's death.

> *[Polonius enters]*
> HAMLET . . . God bless you, sir!
> POLONIUS My lord, the queen would speak with you, and presently.
> HAMLET Do you see yonder cloud that's almost in shape of a camel?
> POLONIUS By th' mass and 'tis, like a camel indeed.
> HAMLET Methinks it is like a weasel.
> POLONIUS It is backed like a weasel.
> HAMLET Or, like a whale?
> POLONIUS Very like a whale.
> HAMLET Then I will come to my mother by and by.

For buffoonery at its height, in a passage too long to be quoted fully here, the gravediggers' scene (V,i) will serve as a perfect instance. The pressures of the play have by this time built up to a nearly unbearable level; and consequently the dialogue between Hamlet and the saucy gravedigger, and the various exuberantly morbid speeches by Hamlet (on death and Yorick's skull and the inglorious end to which greatness inevitably must come), cover a wide range of feeling from hilarity to cosmic melancholy. The extraordinary volatility thus expressed may be seen in the concluding section of this passage:

> HAMLET . . . Prithee, Horatio, tell me one thing.
> HORATIO What's that, my lord?

HAMLET Dost thou think Alexander looked
o' this fashion i'th'earth?

HORATIO E'en so.

HAMLET And smelt so? pah! *[He sets down the
skull]*

HORATIO E'en so, my lord.

HAMLET To what base uses we may return,
Horatio! Why may not imagination trace
the noble dust of Alexander, till 'a find
it stopping a bung-hole?

HORATIO 'Twere to consider too curiously, to
consider so.

HAMLET No, faith, not a jot, but to follow him
thither with modesty enough, and likeli-
hood to lead it; as thus—Alexander died,
Alexander was buried, Alexander re-
turneth to dust, the dust is earth, of earth
we make loam, and why of that loam
whereto he was converted might they not
stop a beer-barrel?

Imperious Caesar, dead and turned to clay,
Might stop a hole to keep the wind away.
Oh, that that earth, which kept the world in awe,
Should patch a wall t'expel the winter's flaw.

Here the graveyard's verbal tomfoolery ends, in revulsion and in ironic wonder at human pretensions. Yet the
language remains buoyant and fanciful in its mordant
mockery, which is sustained by the precarious formal balance: the abrupt rhythms of question and reply; the out-
bursts of lyrically paced prose, witty and morbid at once,
really a form of early free verse—all brought to conclusion
in two rhyming pentameter couplets similar, in their elegiac cleverness, to Jonson's "On My First Son." Once more,
a movement of wild buffoonery, interlaced with notes of

gloomy realism, paves the way for a scene of traumatic recognition and violent emotion: the arrival of Ophelia's
funeral cortège, a complete surprise to Hamlet and also,
dramatically and poetically, a sharp turn in the play.

This shift beautifully illustrates laughter's contribution
to the volatile possibilities of poetry, breaking the spell of
solemnity and allowing unexpected feeling and associations to break through. With the arrival of the cortège, a
purer lyricism takes over, beginning with Hamlet's double
inquiry: "Who is this they follow? / And with such maimèd
rites?" His questions are innocent, yet so imbued with the
scene's death-awareness that their gentle gravity cleanses
away his previous tough-minded manner. The questions,
and the tonal complex they help engender, might well have
given Keats an important stylistic clue for his "Ode on
a Grecian Urn." His own similar questions in the "Ode"
("Who are these coming to the sacrifice? / To what green
altar . . . ?")—together with his succession of richly serious
riddles and oxymora, certainly witty and at times even
worldly—make for a parallel complex of feeling. It is implicit
at the very start, in the image of the urn as a "still unrav-
ished bride of quietness." And further along (to cite just
two obvious instances), the punning on such words as
"brede" and "overwrought" is hardly unconscious. Both
works mix elegiac brooding with a boisterously clever, sexually charged release of imagination.

Wit and sharp wordplay, then, are decisive elements in
all the passages just considered. Even in Keats's poem and
other subtle lyrical writing, their presence is often, however quietly, as telling as in *Hamlet*. Take this untitled poem
of Rainer Maria Rilke's, written in 1913–14.

Du im Voraus
verlorne Geliebte, Nimmergekommene,
nicht weiss ich, welche Töne dir lieb sind.
Nicht mehr versuch ich, dich, wenn das
      Kommende wogt,
zu erkennen. Alle die grossen
Bilder in mir, im Fernen erfahrene Landschaft,
Städte und Türme und Brücken und un-
vermutete Wendung der Wege
und das Gewaltige jener von Göttern
einst durchwachsenen Länder:
steigt zur Bedeutung in mir
deiner, Entgehende, an.

Ach, die Gärten bist du,
ach, ich sah sie mit solcher
Hoffnung. Ein offenes Fenster
im Landhaus—, und du tratest beinahe
mir nachdenklich heran. Gassen fand ich,—
du warst sie gerade gegangen,
und die Spiegel manchmal der Läden der
      Händler
waren noch schwindlich von dir und gaben
      erschrocken
mein zu plötzlich Bild.—Wer weiss, ob derselbe
Vogel nicht hinklang durch uns
gestern, einzeln, im Abend?

[You from the outset
lost beloved, my never-arrived,
I've no idea, none, what tones are dear to you.
No longer do I hope, when the moment wells up,
to recognize you. All the vast
scenes inside me, so far off, so familiar,
cities and towers and bridges and unforeseen winding of ways
and that stormy world where gods

once strode through the lands:
all this within me presses toward one meaning:
you, vanishing.

Oh, the gardens are you,
oh, I saw them with such
yearning. An open window
in the country-house,—and you almost stepped
        forth
to me, bemused. Streets I came upon,—
you had just gone down them,
and sometimes the mirrors in the shops
were still giddy with you and, startled, shot back
my too-sudden reflection.—Who knows, if the
        very same
bird didn't call through us both
separately, yesterday, in the evening?]*

Rilke's poem takes place entirely inwardly. It is addressed to a "beloved" he can never hope to see, an imagined woman who is the essence of everything that fills his subjective existence—indeed, everything visionary and dangerous fed into our psyches by ancient myth and religion. The poem has the tone of romantic longing, but of something more buoyant at the same time. It is vividly specific and surprisingly urban in some of its imagery; cities, towers, bridges, streets and shop-mirrors mingle with god-peopled landscapes and pastoral symbols: gardens, singing birds, a country-house.

Formally, the German is audacious in certain respects, such as its use of adverbs and adjectives as nouns ("im Voraus," "Nimmergekommene," and "das Kommende," for instance—literally, "in the beforehand," "the never-arrived,"

*translation by M.L.R.

and "the oncoming"). The poem is resonant with irregular sound-echoings: far-apart internal rhymes like "Voraus" and "Landhaus," identical ones like the repeated "weiss," subtly varied rhythmic echoes (as in the closing lines of the two verse-units), and a striking number of other such effects for such a short piece. Also, it has shock effects that one can't quite call humorous but are of the same order. An example is the image of the startled mirrors giving the poet his own reflection instead of his beloved's, whom he had so intently imagined passing before them that they became giddy ("schwindlich") with her physical self.

The poem's power is cumulative. What happens in it is a realization made authentic by the immediacy of the beloved's felt presence from the very start. The poem becomes a journey toward her that all but finds her and certainly speaks to her. All the negative notes are themselves concrete images: "lost beloved, my never-arrived," the poet's not knowing "what tones are dear to you," the "open window," where she is all but seen, and the mirror from which her image has disappeared. Playing with the music of anticipation in the face of foregone loss, the poem is pure discovery.

We come now to a drastic phase of such poetic discovery, already suggested in the foregoing discussion. Both the aesthetic deployment of language and the free play of wit in associative process dissolve the restraints of habitual thought, opening the way to explorations beyond the poet's original expectations. Wallace Stevens remarked that "a book of poems is a damned serious thing," and this freeing-up of the mind from its ingrained and ingrown inhibitions is a release into dangerous territory. At a certain pitch of genius, beyond the apprentice (or the simply hopeless) level, a poet does have to write out of the way he or she really— and largely unconsciously—is. This is not a matter of just mirroring one's private self in one's writing; that is not the point at all. Rather, it is a matter of working as best one can out of one's whole state of awareness, from the barely conscious images and moods of reverie to the clearest states of explicit thought. Psychologically, the enterprise can be most perilous.

Ezra Pound, whose gifts I have touched on in the preceding chapter,[1] offers a compelling demonstration. There is not much use, at this late date, in laboring the well-known facts about his politics. He entertained compromised attitudes and indeed—a little as Mayakovsky had done in Russia—attitudinized himself into a corner and associated himself with Mussolini's Fascism, finally escaping trial for treason only by virtue of his supposed insanity.

A complex matter, but we may focus here (without apology for ourselves or for him) on the genius-side of the Pound equation. He was a great poet, not only in his virtuosity but also in the way his art was a reflex of the passion behind his convictions and of his sense of artistic and personal predicament. In his best work, he is unsurpassed in the way his poems give objective form to the inchoate flux of subjective life: a result that is the special triumph of the lyrical as the decisive element in poetry.

Let me cite a relatively early poem of Pound's as illustration, and also as a means of leading into the issue of how the poet's ideology and convictions connect with his art. This is the poem "The Coming of War: Actaeon," first published in March 1915.

[1] See pages 39–45.

THE COMING OF WAR: ACTAEON

An image of Lethe,
        and the fields
Full of faint light
        but golden,
Gray cliffs,
        and beneath them
A sea
Harsher than granite,
        unstill, never ceasing;
High forms
        with the movement of gods,
Perilous aspect;
        And one said:
"This is Actaeon."
        Actaeon of golden greaves!
Over fair meadows,
Over the cool face of that field,
Unstill, ever moving
Hosts of an ancient people,
The silent cortège.

    The poem's title is an unusual gesture—for this poet at any rate—toward explicitly spelling out the psychological pressure underlying its associative complex. Without the title, only a preternaturally suggestible reader could readily see the connection between the poem and the recent outbreak of the Great War, let alone that between the War and Actaeon. But the title nudges us firmly toward these crucial associations and, as it happens, toward the essential nature of poetic process revealed in Pound's development and in the greatest poetry generally. Specifically, the process is one of conversion of private awareness by an artistic medium: the language of lyric poetry, with its melodic dimensions, its partnership with memory, and its love affair with sensation and feeling. This conversion makes the most intimately private, idiosyncratic states available through the plastic, aesthetic medium of language. The more serious and gifted the poet, the greater the risks both of self-exposure and of being carried to disastrous limits. *Immediacy of association (the height of poetic wit) has no defense.*

What has all this to do with "The Coming of War: Actaeon"?

To return to the poem's title, the implied analogy is between two instances of tragic blundering, the one mythical, the other historical: the blundering of Actaeon into Artemis' grove of sacred female mysteries, so that he saw the goddess bathing and was punished by being turned into a stag and torn to death by his own hunting dogs; and the blundering of the nations, once again as countless times before, into war.

The analogy implicit in the title becomes the frame for the poem, which may be compared to a dream-based scenario. It begins in the realm of the dead, with the river Lethe—the river of forgetfulness—flowing through Hades, here merged with the Elysian fields:

> An image of Lethe,
>   and the fields
> Full of faint light
>   but golden.

Eerie, sad, and lovely at once, these lines give a distanced and impersonal yet intense coloration, as of irrevocable loss, to the poem's opening. The coloration grows grimmer and threatening in the next four lines; their starker beauty has a nightmare edge of deadly risk:

> Gray cliffs,
> > and beneath them
> A sea
> Harsher than granite,
> > unstill, never ceasing.

The gathering tonality has something to do with the drastic implications of the death-ridden title. At the same time, the two initial passages I have quoted—while not explicitly linked with one another as pictorially continuous (but metonymically attached)—provide an extended vision of the realm of death not given in Greek myth or in its attendant classical literature. That is, the sea dashing forever against the cliffs appears as the violent, intractable route to death although death's supernatural realm exists high above it. The succession of juxtaposed sentence-fragments is completed by an ambiguous description of god-like figures and a phrase—"Perilous aspect"—that applies equally to their demeanor and to the extended scene itself:

> High forms
> > with the movement of gods,
> Perilous aspect.

It may, for a moment, seem to be pressing things a bit to find, in this unfocused yet commanding imagery, a suggestion of the linked power and terror symbolized in the Actaeon myth and enacted in the very nature of war. Yet suddenly the poem takes a decisive turn to just this suggestion:

> > And one said:
> "This is Actaeon."
> > Actaeon of golden greaves!

This is one of those torques (sharp, unexpected shifts of perspective) that mark Pound's finest work so unmistakably. A voice from within the realm of godlike shades that overlooks the murderous sea has recognized a new arrival: presumably Actaeon after his punishment for having profaned the sacred retreat of Artemis. Then the poem itself cries out the Homeric epithet, "Actaeon of golden greaves!"—an epithet more suitable to a warrior than to a hunter. After this outcry the extended image of the hordes of all the past dead forming a funeral procession for the newest arrival takes over the rest of the poem. In this closing passage, the quiet, impersonal intensity of the opening lines is recaptured and then powerfully deepened by that simultaneously grave and turbulent vision. If we recall the title once more, we shall see Actaeon's arrival as embodying the new deaths of the present war, and the "silent cortège"—the "hosts of an ancient people"—as including all their predecessors in all the wars of history:

> Over fair meadows,
> Over the cool face of that field,
> Unstill, ever moving
> Hosts of an ancient people,
> The silent cortège.

The poem's first line, "An image of Lethe," introduces a particular scene. It also, of course, introduces the whole poem, thus suggesting that part of mankind's blundering into war results from *forgetting* what the past has taught, for the word "Lethe" implies both death and the obliteration of memory. Thus, from the start, the poem begins to evoke a vast, subtle complex of concerns and attitudes related to war, historical memory, fatality, and human limitations. The greatest of our limitations, the Actaeon myth reveals, is that we cannot foresee the consequences of what existential circumstance will drive us into being and doing.

Early on, Pound appears to have been haunted by this myth as a key not only to history but to his own fated personal path as both man and poet. The idea seized him that independent thought and daring association must inevitably lead to unintended sacrilegious intrusions like Actaeon's, for they point to realms of vision and experience that are taboo—that is, are beyond our human ability to deal with or control. Bold artistic exploration must take us away from familiar, approved, safe pathways. Pound's major work reveals an implicit poetics related to what we may call this Actaeon principle: a doomed sense of poetic process as crucially subject to the swerve of the unforeseen, despite the importance to poets of supreme mastery of their art.

Pound comes closest to putting the case explicitly—if elusively—in a passage of Canto 4 (1919). Eight lines in all, it begins with an imagined scene in which the mad Provençal poet Peire Vidal, who like Actaeon is said to have been attacked by his own dogs (when he disguised himself in a wolfskin), is

> Stumbling, stumbling along in the wood,
> Muttering, muttering Ovid:
>   "Pergusa . . . pool . . . pool . . . Gargaphia,
> "Pool . . . pool of Salmacis."

As if he were Pound himself, Vidal is dreaming of scenes and transformations in Ovid's *Metamorphoses,* at once miraculous and shot through with a sort of doomed sexuality: the ravishment of Persephone near the lake Pergusa; Actaeon's tragic arrival at Gargaphia, sacred to Artemis; and the misfortunes of Hermaphroditus because of the water-nymph Salmacis. Then, in the same verse-unit but no longer in Vidal's supposed voice, the single line "The empty armour shakes as the cygnet moves" evokes the escape of Neptune's son Cygnus in the form of a swan when Achilles was about to slay him. The line, exquisite in itself and ominously resonant, serves as a transition to three lines suggesting the uncontrollable context of artistic vision, seen in the metaphor of liquid light introduced by the troubadour Arnaut Daniel (and translated by Pound alongside it at the beginning of the new verse-unit):

> Thus the light rains, thus pours, *e lo soleills plovil*
> The liquid and rushing crystal
> > beneath the knees of the gods.

Beauty is thus subtly related to unseen powers, and creation to tragic risk or error. Pound's larger identification in the *Cantos* as a whole is with Odysseus, who constantly ran the risk of the unknown. Actaeon and Vidal are minor alternatives to the Odyssean model, shading it toward a personal and tragic coloration—an emphasis on humiliation and remorse rather than sheer archaic heroism. The *Cantos* present scattered notes of self-reproach, as if written by a remorseful and introspective Odysseus, and pointedly recall that not even he had "care and craft" enough to forestall all folly. Sometimes, they express a piercing regret for a failure of compassion (perhaps the result of rigorous artistic shunning of sentimentality):

> Les larmes que j'ai creées m'inondent
> Tard, très tard je t'ai connue, la Tristesse,
> I have been hard as youth sixty years.

Such an insight confesses recognition that one has imperceptibly grown into a disastrous, perhaps irrevocable state, even if out of originally good or innocent motives. This is the gist of what I have called the Actaeon principle or factor: the inevitable blundering into violation of the forbidden that attends a persistently free, exploring, uninhibited imagination. Thus Pound at his worst can, with a certain power of genuine feeling, utter a note of vile racism. An utterance of this kind represents what I would consider the greatest risk of passionate alertness in and out of art: a risk Pound perceived but could not altogether cope with.

The contradiction between his blundering into a moral morass and the sheer pleasure afforded by the poetry I have been quoting has led me into the old "Pound question" for a moment, but in a special poetic context. The quotations reveal the infinite seductiveness of artistic mastery and the helpless candor toward which it draws the artist—that is, the clarifying of associations at work in the depths of reverie. This kind of mastery is not so much technical skill alone, although such skill is almost always inseparable from poetic gifts when they are at all developed. To have such gifts is to enjoy the innate plasticity of language and therefore to feel an uncommon fascination with its sounds, rhythms, silences, and suggestive resonances—in themselves and as openings into the associative process that promises unforeseeable revelations.

The few quotations by Pound offered in this and the preceding chapter share a richly engaging poetic music given body by an extraordinarily moving and intense phrasing, fraught with a sense of "perilous aspect." This is true as well of the work by Jonson, Marvell, Shakespeare, and Rilke I have been discussing, work representative of the most serious poetic artistry. The implication, always

challenging and disturbing, is that beauty in art is a reciprocal of the simultaneously seductive and terrifying flux of
human existence, so full of ambiguities and of opposed
states of feeling. Childlike delight in sheer perception goes
hand in hand, repeatedly, with disillusion or awakened
fatalism. Thus, Elizabeth Bishop's "Five Flights Up" is at
once full of lively and even charmed observation and bur-
dened with a dark, heavy irony:

> Still dark.
> The unknown bird sits on his usual branch.
> The little dog next door barks in his sleep
> inquiringly, just once.
> Perhaps in his sleep, too, the bird inquires
> once or twice, quavering.
> Questions—if that is what they are—
> answered directly, simply,
> by day itself.
>
> Enormous morning, ponderous, meticulous;
> gray light streaking each bare branch,
> each single twig, along one side,
> making another tree, of glassy veins . . .
> The bird still sits there. Now he seems to yawn.
>
> The little black dog runs in his yard.
> His owner's voice arises, stern,
> "You ought to be ashamed!"
> What has he done?
> He bounces cheerfully up and down;
> He rushes in circles in the fallen leaves.
>
> Obviously, he has no sense of shame.
> He and the bird know everything is answered,
> all taken care of,
> no need to ask again.
> —Yesterday brought to today so lightly!
> (A yesterday I find almost impossible to lift.)

In the first three verse-units, the bird and the little dog are more or less center-stage and somewhat humanized as mildly comic, quite lovable innocents. Certain notes, though, prevent sheer gleefulness of tone. The first line, in fact, is a condensed elliptical sentence that opens the poem most emphatically within a state of lingering darkness. The second line introduces the bird a little mysteriously and perhaps with a slight touch of weariness ("The unknown bird sits on his usual branch"), forestalling any sense that the poem will be all charmed whimsy. These initial impressions are reinforced by the thoughtful, gently envious closing sentence of this first unit. Then, in a long awestruck phase, the next unit describes the late-autumn daybreak as "enormous" and "ponderous" and also, because of the eerie double outline its "gray light" imposes on the tree, "meticulous" in its strangeness.

The third unit, it is true, is all bounce and warmth despite the word "stern" (used humorously here) and the reminder at the end of "fallen leaves." But in the closing verse-unit the poem's accumulated irony crystallizes. The unthinking certainties of bird and dog, or indeed any lighthearted view of time and of the promise of a new day—of "Questions . . . / answered directly, simply"—are seen as totally naive in the two final lines, which may also imply that the massive weight of yesterday includes some "shame" (since earlier on the poem has played a bit insistently on this word). The reversal of mood is striking, of course, after the gaiety of the scene with the little dog.

The mixture of tones in "Five Flights Up," and its gathering cloud of sardonic gloom (muted though it is in the interest of avoiding self-pitying lugubriousness), are characteristic in the structure of a great many of the best lyric poems. It is as if delight itself were an Actaeon-like blunder we fall into, disastrously, through sheer, helpless absorption in the moment's impermanent loveliness or its other magnetic qualities. A more powerful instance is Emily Dickinson's poem #258, with its fused ravishment and pain. It begins abruptly, with a brilliant image whose lyrical impact recalls, in its beauty and sadness, the passage in *Hamlet* beginning "There is a willow grows aslant a brook"; and it ends with a chilled image of mortality:

> There's a certain Slant of light,
> Winter Afternoons—
> That oppresses, like the Heft
> Of Cathedral Tunes—
>
> Heavenly Hurt, it gives us—
> We can find no scar,
> But internal difference,
> Where the Meanings, are—
>
> None may teach it—Any—
> 'Tis the Seal Despair—
> An imperial affliction
> Sent us of the Air—
>
> When it comes, the Landscape listens—
> Shadows—hold their breath—
> When it goes, 'tis like the Distance
> On the look of Death—

"Where the Meanings, are—!" No critical statement could convey better than this line, in the context of this poem, the a-logical, emotionally charged character of the "meanings" conveyed by works of art. In any case, this is a marvelous line in a marvelous poem. It points directly to that realm of "internal difference" where our subjective sense of "the Meanings" dwells. This is the realm that poetry objectifies through its lyrical dynamics (shifting tonalities and degrees of intensity, which are given structure and subtle shading through the resonance and interweaving of sounds and images and key phrases).

To trace the process in Dickinson's poem is to follow the deepening of an already complex pressure of feeling. The bemused expression "a certain Slant of Light"—in which "Slant" implies a possibly disturbed awareness—starts off an indirect association, of a sort so elusive that much of it goes on below surface-consciousness. (It might well have begun with the slanting light coming through a church window, although in the poem itself the line gives us an outdoors image.) Next, the heavy, cold implications of "Winter Afternoons" and the words "oppresses" and "Heft" confirm the disturbance as a weight on the spirit, one nevertheless ennobled by the sacred associations of "Cathedral tunes" and "Heavenly" and the splendor of "imperial."

These associations and others flow into the fear-laden personifications, culminating in the image of "the look of Death," in the final stanza. The most emotion-charged single words ("oppresses," "Hurt," "Despair," and "Death") follow on one another with increasingly drastic effect, with the last two strategically placed in the rhyme-scheme for maximum emphasis. All we had at the start was the sense of the angle of sunlight on a winter afternoon. That is what we still have at the end, but it has taken on the weight of tragic knowledge of inevitable defeat in the making: "the Seal Despair" that so often waits upon innocent action or perception and is the affective name of the Actaeon factor.

FOUR

The Clear, Elusive Poem-in-Itself

The preceding chapters have assumed the human seriousness of poetic art, which coexists with its pleasures and is
in fact enhanced by them. Emily Dickinson's phrase
"Heavenly Hurt" touches the issue exactly, and Pound's
use of the Actaeon legend beautifully embodies it. Both
are striking clues to the psychological pressures linking
private sensibility, public meaning, and artistic expression.
We know we are not free agents and that each of us is in
one sense a representative person. But neither are we
automatons or mere statistical units; every shared social
concern, every individual man or woman, every creative
act has surprising dimensions and is irreducible to formu-
las. Thus, while poetry has to do with matters of central
importance to us all, it resists translation into set positions.

A quick second glance at a few poems discussed earlier
on will illustrate. Yeats's "The Tower" quite obviously pre-

sents the predicaments of old age. Edward Thomas's "As
the team's head brass" copes with the prospect of becoming a war casualty. Philip Larkin's "High Windows" confronts (and represents) the cynicism and spiritual emptiness
induced by the falling away of past religious and moral
assumptions. Marvell's "The Picture of Little T.C. in a
Prospect of Flowers" reflects the helpless anguish of people in a time of widespread child mortality. Emily Dickinson's "There's a certain Slant of light" sees, even in something apparently so irrelevant as the angle of sunlight on
a winter afternoon, the encroachment of death on our
minds and spirits. These are moving and disturbing subjects, yet hardly original in themselves. They do not define
the special qualities of the poems just listed; those qualities
lie elsewhere.

Poems have a way of avoiding entrapment by their
starting points. But even their starting points cannot really
be stated in thematic terms. Yeats's poem, for instance, starts
out in a frenzy of self-exposing absurdity far more humil-
iated and comically desperate than any geriatrician's scientific study could begin to convey. It mobilizes ever wider
and wilder ranges of association and contrast—worlds of
memory, fantasy, defiance, and deep questioning—before
it finally projects a state of desire for self-anaesthesis against
all the griefs of loss, remorse, and decrepitude. One needs
to submit to its orchestrated dynamics, almost as if to music,
in order to grasp it clearly: the successive colorations and
intensities, the sudden shifts, the tonal interactions, the
cumulative volatility, and then the stripping down of feeling.

So too with the other poems I have mentioned. Each
one engages with a particular situation or emotional cir-

cumstance but is from the start free of anything like discursive development. Edward Thomas's poem moves from
the impression of a typical scene and a random encounter
during a country walk to an atmosphere of heavy spiritual
depression and muted horror. The manner in which grimness breaks through the surface of casual, humorous detachment is the unique fingerprint of this poem's idiom.
Similarly, the growth in Larkin's poem from raucously vulgar commentary to rueful ironies to lyrical melancholy could
not be predicted by locating the general subject.

Far more daring than either of these poems, Marvell's
leaps from one extreme tonal complex—the playful courtly
adoration and even deification of a baby girl—to sheer
terror of almost primitive force. This torque of feeling
is matched by the rapid movement in Emily Dickinson's
"There's a certain Slant of light," perhaps the purest of
our examples in its concentrated deepening. Starting with
an isolated visual and atmospheric perception of a physical
phenomenon, it ends by confronting "the look of death"
in all its impersonal finality. In between, it hovers for a few
lines over the place "Where the Meanings, are"—the site
of "internal difference" (the "scar" left from the wound of
a consciousness awakened to death's reality). The "Meanings" are unspecified logically or philosophically; the poem
stresses only its awareness of their presence. If its bearing
were at all like that of discourse, it would certainly dwell
here on just what they are. It speeds immediately onward,
however, following through the associations set in motion
by the "certain Slant of light." Interestingly, the associative
chain's climactic completion also provides a release from
the process that has led to it. Chiefly through the word
"Distance," the poem opens outward into a feeling of pure

abandonment to nothingness once the "Slant of light" ceases to dominate it:

> When it comes, the Landscape listens—
> Shadows—hold their breath—
> When it goes, 'tis like the Distance
> On the look of Death—

Was there something reassuring, after all, in the brief lingering of that "Slant" epiphany which chillingly recalled such grim "Meanings"—a promise that death was still only imminent, and not yet irreversible? The poem does not say. It is not concerned with explanations—only with phrasing that will evoke clear but untranslatable states of feeling and awareness. Art of this sort is hardly devoid of thought or moral import, but these cannot limit its reach. The poetic process converts them into lyric, malleable tonal elements: awed or thoughtful gravity, say, or glowing piety, or gentle compassion, or fiery outrage. The language of poetry is a volatile medium, charged with subjective resonances that include the emotional dimensions and tentative aspects of intellectual activity. The meaning of a poem, then, lies in its affective structure.

Much of this is true as well of ordinary speech, which shares with poetry the implicit rationale of language itself: the urge to convey the whole feeling, or body of subjective meaning, that is our human matrix of observation and experience. It is this urge that compels infants to strive for speech so vigorously and that makes us skeptical of purportedly objective accounts of reality, and even of the existence of realities outside our personal experience. It is not hard, then, to see that the tonal structures of poetry are vitally central in genuine communication. They are adventures in catching hold of insights and following them wherever they lead. With every nuance or abrupt turn, they evoke the complexity and shadings of the streams of elusive felt truth we are forever encountering.

In light of these considerations, it is interesting to read a passage from the memoirs of the poet Boris Pasternak on the suicides of certain authors—men and women who were his contemporaries and had shared with him the excitement of the Russian Revolution and then its disheartening aftermath.[1] One sees, through the thick glass of translation, that the character of this passage in the original must lie somewhere between earnest conversation and prose-poetry. The passage is a special instance of poetic perspective (absent an actual poem, of course) on reality and its meanings. It begins by drawing a distinction between the mental states of people being tortured to death and of people about to commit suicide:

> We have no idea of the mental agony that precedes suicide. Under physical torture on the rack, people lose consciousness every minute, the sufferings inflicted . . . being so great that they bring the end near by the very fact of being so unendurable. Subjected to torture by a hangman, a man is not yet utterly destroyed; though unconscious from pain, he is nevertheless present at his own end, his past belongs to him, his memories are with him, and . . . may be of some use to him before he dies.
> Having arrived at the thought of suicide,

[1] Boris Pasternak, *I Remember: Sketch for an Autobiography,* trans. David Magarshack (New York: Pantheon, 1959), pp. 88–90.

one abandons all hope, one turns away from
one's past, one declares oneself a bankrupt
and one's memories as non-existent. These
memories are no longer capable of reaching
the would-be suicide to . . . sustain him. The
continuity of one's inner existence is
destroyed, the personality has ceased to exist.
In the end, perhaps, one kills oneself . . .
because one can no longer endure the agony
that does not seem to belong to anyone in
particular, . . . the empty suspense . . . not
filled up by a life that still goes on.

This is not mere speculation. It reflects literal knowledge of the experience of five people (the novelist Fadeyev
and the poets Mayakovsky, Esenin, Tsvetayeva, and Yashvili) and of the brutalities of the Stalin era. The talk of
torture, hanging, and suicide is not melodramatic but existential. At the same time, the repeated word "memories"
provides a surprising emphasis, one that only a poet would
be likely to impose. Memories, so important in the making
of a poem, are conceived as also essential to one's sense of
human identity, which poetry embodies *par excellence*. The
torturer's victim has them as a sole resource for self-reas-
surance and comfort. The suicide, on the other hand, has
lost touch with memories—or deliberately abandoned
them—and thus has allowed "the continuity of inner existence [to be] destroyed," so that "the personality has ceased
to exist."

We could find no bolder or more serious expression
anywhere of the assumption that the inner sources of poetry
are indistinguishable from those of meaningful life generally. Pasternak goes on to give his five tragic instances:
the cases of writers who could not handle the pressure of

the times and either betrayed their integrity knowingly or became, out of sheer confusion and horrified despair, devoid of memory and identity:

> Mayakovsky shot himself out of pride because he had condemned something in himself or around himself with which his self-respect could not be reconciled. Esenin hanged himself without any clear realization of the consequences . . . Marina Tsvetayeva all her life shielded herself by her work against the humdrum affairs of everyday existence. When it seemed to her that it was an inadmissible luxury and for the sake of her son she must for a time sacrifice her all-absorbing passion, she cast a sober look around her and she saw the chaos that had not filtered through her creative work, immovable, stagnant, monstrous, and recoiled in panic. Not knowing how to protect herself from that horror, she hurriedly hid herself in death, putting her head into a noose as under a pillow. I can't help feeling that Paolo Yashvili was no longer capable of comprehending anything at all when . . . he gazed at his sleeping daughter at night and imagined he was no longer worthy of looking at her and in the morning went to his comrades and blew out his brains with the shot from his double-barrelled gun. And it seems to me that Fadeyev, with that guilty smile which he managed to preserve through all the cunning intricacies of politics, could bid farewell to himself at the last moment before pulling the trigger with, I should imagine, words like these "Well, it's all over! Good-bye, Sasha!"

✓ Freedom of the imagination is the oxygen of poetry. The sense of limitless possibilities and directions is indispensable. But personal memories, and with them the mind's quick linkings of disparate perceptions, events, and images, give poems their organic physicality. In circumstances of murderous repression, the full import of the imagination's need for full, deep, unsupervised breathing grows brilliantly clear as the supreme value that it is. Pasternak's thoughts are a rare revelation of the crucial seriousness of what poets must do, each in his or her own unhampered way, and of the close kinship of their task to the basic meanings of human existence and integrity.

Needless to say, it took every ounce of strength for the poets named by Pasternak, and for himself and many others as well, to keep breathing by writing in their own way. Compromise by writing politically acceptable poems of a "heroic" or sentimentally idealistic nature was the most obvious danger. Mayakovsky had had his period of such writing before he returned to his true bent and found himself in the state Pasternak describes. Yashvili and Fadeyev, lesser talents, could not return to themselves even in the complex way that Mayakovsky did. Others, however, simply found it impossible to adjust to external demands. The fine, unconscious train of association, nuance, and truthfulness to actual impressions and feelings could not allow for such adjustment, except possibly in a negative way.

An example of this last kind of response is Osip Mandelstam's famous poem about Stalin, which led to his arrest in 1934 and subsequent persecution until his death four years later. According to his translator, Robert Tracy, he "suffered from a kind of writers' block between 1925 and

1930. . . . He had already discovered that many journals were unwilling to publish his work, presumably because of his traditional humanist values and his failure to celebrate the new Soviet regime with conspicuously patriotic verse."[2] Here is the poem on Stalin, in Tracy's translation:

> We live, but we do not feel the land beneath us;
> Ten steps away and our words cannot be heard,
>
> And when there are just enough people for half a
>   dialogue—
> Then they remember the Kremlin mountaineer.
>
> His fat fingers are slimy, like slugs,
> And his words are absolute, like grocers' weights.
>
> His cockroach whiskers are laughing,
> And his boot-tops shine.
>
> He has a rabble of skinny-necked leaders around
>   him,
> He plays games with the aid of those who are only
>   half human,
>
> Who twitter, who mew, who whimper.
> He alone bangs and thrusts.
>
> Decree after decree, he hammers them out like
>   horseshoes—
> One in the groin for him, in the forehead for him,
>   one in the eyes for him.
>
> When he has an execution it's a special treat
> And the Ossetian chest swells.

At first the poem seems pure vituperation. But even in this translated version we can see other elements of its dynamics at work. It begins in an atmosphere of total iso-

[2] *Osip Mandelstam's "Stone,"* translated and with an introduction by Robert Tracy (Princeton: Princeton University Press, 1981), pp. 10, 12.

lation: "We" live without communication and in a paralysis of fear. ("We" are all the inhabitants of the country, considered as potentially independent sensibilities.) Then the third and fourth couplets project both revulsion and recognition of blunt, arrogant power, describing Stalin in images of subhuman grossness: "slugs," "cockroach." Next, his henchmen are introduced as equally subhuman, but in language more expressive of contempt than of sheer primal disgust and fear: tones reserved only for Stalin and his power. The final two couplets return to him, focusing on his relentless, iron cruelty that finds something like climactic ecstasy in ordering executions.

Subtler dimensions reveal themselves as well. The first two lines (or, alternatively, the first two couplets) might stand alone as a poem of bitter complaint. Thereafter, though, the satiric attack begins, with each couplet—and indeed, almost every line—a counterblow to the decrees that Stalin "hammers . . . out like horseshoes." Also, the poem assumes our grasp of its context: that these are words uttered amidst literal isolation and danger, gathering into a considerable act of courage. (Mandelstam recited them to a small group of supposed friends, one of whom was apparently an informer.) Among the poem's interesting aspects is the fact that Stalin is not named. The poem *pretends* to be exercising caution by indirection but of course does nothing of the sort. Every detail, including references to his "Ossetian" background (in the mountainous North Caucasus), points directly to the ruler in the Kremlin.

In yet another sense, the poem's affective movement is a mirror image, from the opposite standpoint, of what it is attacking. Thus, it begins with immersion in a state of remoteness: that of the sequestered victim rather than of the unapproachable tyrant. Then it moves into a barely hinted state of pride in belonging to a tiny, muffled elite (as opposed to the pride of power) and breaks into an extended song of disdain for the rulers. Finally, it mimics the enemy's thrusts of heartless violence, growing into a chant of hatred that turns Stalin's own qualities into verbal missiles against him—and just possibly against enduring life itself any further. There is no glimmer of hope in the poem; and Stalin's thrill of joy in ordering executions is matched by an exulting bitterness, possibly masochistic and suicidal, in the ferocity of Mandelstam's ironic assault.

By an obvious turn of association, these thoughts have suddenly reminded me of a poem by the American writer James Dickey—his vivid "Deer among Cattle." Despite their obvious differences, I think the connection between Dickey's and Mandelstam's poems should be clear.

> Here and there in the searing beam
> Of my hand going through the night meadow
> They all are grazing
>
> With pins of human light in their eyes.
> A wild one also is eating
> The human grass,
>
> Slender, graceful, domesticated
> By darkness, among the bred-
> for-slaughter,
>
> Having bounded their paralyzed fence
> And inclined his branched forehead onto
> Their green frosted table,
>
> The only live thing in this flashlight
> Who can leave whenever he wishes,
> Turn grass into forest,

Foreclose inhuman brightness from his eyes
But stands here still, unperturbed,
In their wide-open country,

The sparks from my hand in his pupils
Unmatched anywhere among cattle,

Grazing with them the night of the hammer
As one of their own who shall rise.

Now, "Deer among Cattle" has a far gentler surface than the poem on Stalin. And yet, just suppose it had been written in the USSR in the early 1930s, under the circumstances Pasternak describes. Perhaps no one would have paid any attention—that most common experience of Western poets—except other poets and the most literate readers. But ideological scrutiny would have been extremely likely, and the ordinary first response would have been to read a suspect if not a totally hostile symbolism into the piece. The free-moving deer, "a wild one," could well have been taken as signifying advocacy of undisciplined individualism, the doomed cattle as a hostile representation of the Russian people's condition, and the ending as a prediction of their counterrevolutionary insurrection. And if it happened that slow-witted ideologues, unresponsive at times to such possible nuances, failed to take notice, then dissidents—from their opposite standpoint—would be sure to do so. How else, for instance, would Mandelstam have read Dickey's lines, even though a poet of his caliber would have responded to their primary qualities as well?

Moreover, Dickey's poem does after all point strongly to something like political meaning: the difference between free choice and a life of what Thoreau called "quiet desperation." The phrase "bred- / for-slaughter" and the language of the closing couplet add violent emphasis to this

distinction. (The word "hammer" and its brutal implications here accidentally echo Mandelstam.) The whole tone
of bitter yet visionary arousal implies more than mere opposition to animal slaughter; by no great stretch of imagination, one might read opposition to war and even to con-
scription into the poem.

These "meanings" do suggest themselves, whether
sharply or only penumbrally. Yet essentially the poem is
touched off by the converging memories of two unusual
experiences: coming upon grazing cattle, caught in the glare
of one's flashlight, at night; and seeing a lone deer among
them. The primary effect throughout is simply of strangeness, made palpable by the "night meadow" vision just
mentioned. Superimposed on this innermost body of the
poem are the possibly "political" resonances I have also
noted. These are reinforced by other touches at strategic
points along the way. For instance, "searing beam" implies
from the start that man is *the* enemy. Later, we have "pins
of human light in their eyes," "bred- / for-slaughter,"
"paralyzed fence," "inhuman brightness," "the sparks from
my hand," and "night of the hammer."

What we are given, then, is the fascination of an unusual
moment, complicated by the observer's ambivalent role and
by the strongly hinted anarcho-bohemian-misanthropic
attitude that becomes emphatic at the end. These moral
and political implications are kept from overwhelming the
poem by the stronger impact of the initial scene, but a severe
consideration of Dickey's poem would find them too explicit
and insistent nevertheless: a poetic, not a political criticism. They even press the poem into an apparent self-con-
tradiction in the phrase "inhuman brightness." The whole
burden of feeling has been against the inherent ruthless-

ness of man the butcher-species, with his searing technol-
ogy and murderous "hammer," and "inhuman" in this
context would mean "good." True, this may well have been
Dickey's point, with the deer's "inhuman" reflection of the
light standing for a free and therefore *non*-human brightness of being. But the effect, if so intended, is forced. In
any case, the opening nine lines do all the work needed to
suggest the special mixture of surprise, glory, pity,
strangeness, and existential contrast that is the poem's
essence. Despite a certain kinship of implication, Dickey's
poem does not breathe the same atmosphere as Mandelstam's—neither that of helpless oppression, revulsion, and
anger nor that of dangerous transcendence through ironic
empathy.

"Deer among Cattle" has a genuine but limited authority that is all but overborne by its straining after prophetic
wisdom. As a sad result, its free-verse tercets, so crisply
patterned and concretely focused at first, lose momentum
and grow ragged after the ninth line. I would surmise that
Dickey, sensing the loss of momentum, shifted for that
reason to the more compressed couplets that end the poem.
Nevertheless, he crammed the final couplet with an awk-
wardly ambiguous symbolic phrasing, which might equally
refer to proletarian revolution, the resurrection of Jesus,
the promise of some future triumph of humanitarian
decencies, or simply the fact that the deer will bound back
over the fence and leave the cattle's Mandelstam-world.

The poem's weakening takes place at all levels: rhythm,
tonal clarity, and simple perspective. But in its defense one
might say that it has almost inadvertently encountered
something intractable. The man with the flashlight (exactly
why was he there at night?) has come upon the momentar-

ily juxtaposed worlds of the free-moving deer (had the man been hunting?) and the cattle about to be slaughtered. The triple confrontation is indeed fraught with all the insoluble moral and political implications one can think of. The poet, of course, could have chosen to restrain his impulse toward portentous suggestion; but once the "bred- / for-slaughter" reality had been dropped into the stream of awareness, it would have been hard to continue without taking it further into account. Had the poem been allowed to stop at that point, and therefore been contained within nine lines, a brave and fine solution would have been reached. But alas! the poet chose not to rest on this too-little-prized laurel and kept pressing further, until the process went out of control. In a curious sense, this may have been the best possible expression of the intrinsic bafflement of perspective the poem had stumbled into.

To return to the theme of free poetic imagination: as we have seen, it is a matter of carrying through in the wake of an initial impulse without being trapped by one's starting point. That is, there is a conversion process involved between the pang of impulse that marks perception of the stuff of a poem and the poem's actual birth and development. The first impulse is often visual, as with Dickinson's "Slant of light" or Dickey's flashlight view of the deer grazing among the cattle. It can be contrastive, as in Mandelstam's juxtaposing of his isolated and terrified "we" and his savagely caricatured Stalin. And of course there are many other stimulants: a sudden mood or memory, a sense-impression, an incident or situation of any kind. Meanwhile, the process is driven by psychological pressures that command the way surface impulses will be selected and absorbed into poems. Dickinson's highly sensitized awareness of death's constant imminence is one example; Mandelstam's desperately outraged hatred is another. Dickey's confusedly alerted feelings of guilt and excitement are not quite of the same order. They do not constitute a powerful pressure seeking a momentary resolution in the same way; that is one reason that the poem would have been better off simply presenting the scene that led to such a state of imaginative arousal.

Despite some of the language I have just used, I do not mean to imply that one should turn to biography or to poets' statements of intention in gauging the psychological pressure at work in a poem. That pressure reveals itself in the character of the poem itself. It is always idiosyncratically derivable from the poem's own language and structure, never from a generalized deduction from other sources. This is true because, although there is obviously an intimate relationship between a poet's writings and the rest of his or her life, that relationship is never a simple matter—as the poems themselves show. Add to this fact the self-evident one that it is lyric poetry that gives us the most precise expression of psychological and emotional states, and the conclusion should be clear—namely, that it is both revelatory and self-contained. The affective life of a poem is both its whole character and its whole purpose or reason for existing. The psychological pressure that we find within it is its connection with the rest of life. That is why the dynamics of its structure, the shifting relationships of feeling and intensity among its successive units, are not "merely" theoretical considerations but something a great deal more vital and relevant than is generally understood.

Let me try to illustrate through a debatable example,

Walt Whitman's Civil War poem "A Sight in Camp in the Daybreak Gray and Dim":

> A sight in camp in the daybreak gray and dim,
> As from my tent I emerge so early sleepless,
> As slow I walk in the cool fresh air the path near
>   by the hospital tent,
> Three forms I see on stretchers lying, brought out
>   there untended lying,
> Over each the blanket spread, ample brownish
>   woolen blanket,
> Gray and heavy blanket, folding, covering all.
>
> Curious I halt and silent stand,
> Then with light fingers I from the face of the
>   nearest the first just lift the blanket;
> Who are you elderly man so gaunt and grim, with
>   well-gray'd hair, and flesh all sunken about
>   the eyes?
> Who are you my dear comrade?
>
> Then to the second I step—and who are you my
>   child and darling?
> Who are you sweet boy with cheeks yet blooming?
>
> Then to the third—a face nor child nor old, very
>   calm, as of beautiful yellow-white ivory;
> Young man I think I know you—I think this face
>   is the face of the Christ himself,
> Dead and divine and brother of all, and here
>   again he lies.

I call this poem "debatable" only because it can clearly move readers on grounds having little to do with its accomplishment as a work of art. The mere *subject* of the dead in war stirs powerful emotions. Also, if we happen to be aware of the fact (unmentioned in the poem) that Whitman served as a volunteer nurse with the Union army, that knowledge will surely enhance our sense of an elegiac compassion free of any partisan feeling. And the closing references to Christ are in no sense sectarian but purely and climactically humane.

Even if presented in the somewhat trite prose of commonplace oratory, these points of reference could not but move us. For this poem, however, they are forceful springboards of energy but hardly define the resulting structure of feeling, whose deeper pressures and perceptions cannot be so easily classified. Within the long first sentence that constitutes the opening verse-unit, for instance, there is a dynamic movement only tangentially related to any generalities of subject and attitude. The first three lines start the poem off on a quiet personal note, delicately balancing almost imperceptible opposites. Thus, it is "daybreak" (normally something to welcome) but also "gray and dim." Similarly, "I emerge so early" (normally, something quite wholesome) and yet "I" am "sleepless"—presumably because of tension and concern over wounded soldiers as "I walk in the cool fresh air the path near by the hospital tent."

Suddenly, in this same sentence and verse-unit, the physical movement stops and the tone shifts abruptly at the sight of "three forms on stretchers lying . . . untended." This happens in a single line of naked recognition. Then, immediately and compulsively, attention focuses in the final three lines on the heavy blankets enfolding and concealing the dead men. The tone becomes incantatory, with the word "blanket" repeated in each phrase so that it becomes obsessive: a verbal hold against hysteria. At the same time, the diction includes both dismal and reassuring resonances; the "brownish" blankets seem "gray and heavy" but also "ample" and "folding" and "covering all." The gloom and oppression of this magnetic chant are somewhat tempered by subtle hints of intimately tender feeling and of mystery, just barely given in the words I have called reassuring. These hints point to something unexpected—to some revelation of private preoccupations yet to come.

It is not long in coming. The very first lines of the next verse-unit give us yet another important turn. They are introduced by the word "curious" and at once present a state of *transfixed curiosity,* followed by actions attendant upon this state: namely, lifting the blankets to uncover the faces of the dead soldiers, asking the first two an unanswerable question ("Who are you?"), and then projecting an encompassing answer in relation to the third. Each soldier is given his separate verse-unit. The first of these is the grimmest, with a description closest to that of a death's-head, although the elderly corpse is nevertheless addressed as "my dear comrade." The second, brief as a verse-epitaph in the *Greek Anthology,* is all poignant affection. The third solemnly exalts the "young man" addressed as a reimbodiment of the crucified Christ, "dead and divine and brother of all." And with this startling yet appropriate image the poem ends.

In all this process the poem has sloughed off any similarity to standard rhetoric, becoming a unique formation. The language used for the soldiers verges on the unbecoming or embarrassing in its fascination with the dead bodies and its nearly homoerotic intensities of expression. By the end of the poem it is clear that the dead are not heroes in the jingoistic sense or even in a sturdily patriotic sense, but cherished *victims*—the victims of war itself: something the associative movement has carried the accumulated feeling to suggest despite Whitman's belief in the cause of the Union. They are admired and loved and apotheosized as sacrificed love-objects: a sublimation of what otherwise might seem vulgar and, perhaps, sexually morbid prying. Poetically, the movement is far from rhetoric. It starts off with an uneasy balance of fresh morning tones and drearier ones, comes quickly upon the stark scene of the blanket-shrouded dead and hovers prayerfully over the forever muted mystery of their identity, and then boldly (though "with light fingers") probes the mystery and stares into the three unresponsive yet revelatory faces. The aestheticization of the third face ("as of beautiful yellow-white ivory") foreshadows "decadent" tendencies in literature that were to emerge later in the nineteenth century. It follows naturally from the ardent pair of lines addressed to the "sweet boy" of the preceding unit; and both closing units stand in striking relationship to the longer verse-units they follow, which are sunk deep in their mesmerized absorption with physical death itself.

We must back off a bit from this close-up of the sequence of tonalities at work in the shaping of Whitman's poem— as one might from a painting in order to view it in full perspective. We can then see the poem as a complex of literal impressions, starting with the clear descriptions at the beginning, and of successive inward reorientations thereafter. A musing sensibility is rapidly established; it moves directly toward horror, partly concealed, and proceeds to uncover it. After the first shock, it copes with the intractable through the language of love, art, and Christianity. The intellectual implications are ambiguous, but the pigments and varied contexts of feeling sharply clarify a state of fey death-curiosity, an appalled sense of reality, and the summoning up of all available resources to avoid dropping into an abyss of desolation. The abyss remains—

it is the dead, not the risen, Christ who is seen at the end—
and the poem's task is to acknowledge it without illusions
but without surrender of morale.

A NOTE ON TERMINOLOGY,
AND AN ILLUSTRATION

We should not confuse poetry with rhetoric, the art of
persuasion. According to Aristotle, rhetoric entails logical
argument, enhanced by devices for suggesting a speaker's
special authority and for moving listeners emotionally
toward favoring an opinion or a line of action. A poem
may well use the elements of rhetoric, but will subordinate
them to its affective unfolding: the right true mark of its
being a poem and not a piece of discourse. It moves, we
have seen, by association and other subjective resonances,
and also melodically. At this point, and at the risk of our
discussion's being sicklied o'er with the pale cast of peda-
gogy, it may be useful to suggest certain key terms and definitions helpful in following a poem as a living organic
construct.[3]

The first of these terms, not surprisingly, is *poem*, which
may be defined as a projection, by means of compressed
and patterned language, of specific qualities and intensities of emotionally and sensuously charged awareness. As
a work of art using language as its plastic medium, it is not
discourse but an effort to reveal life at the pitch of realization; that is, it objectifies subjective states. A poem's
character does not depend on continuous narration or the

---

[3] These terms and definitions were developed in collaboration with Dr. Sally M.
Gall in the course of preparing our book *The Modern Poetic Sequence: The Genius
of Modern Poetry* (New York: Oxford University Press, 1983) and other studies.
They reflect a need for a vocabulary that has to do, as simply as possible, with
the poetics implicit in poetic practice and in actual poems.

working out of a dramatic situation or a developed argument, but on the felt relationships among its radiating lyric centers—that is, on its lyrical structure.

In turn, we may define a *lyric center* as the basic or radiating unit of poetic structure: a specific quality, and intensity, of emotionally and sensuously charged awareness, residing in the *language of a passage* rather than in the author's supposed feelings or those of a supposed "speaker." A lyric center is in no sense a theme—except in the musically related sense—or a concept or an idea. Alternative terms for lyric center arc *tonal center* and *affect.* The latter term, useful for its psychological overtone, is valuable because it suggests both a subjective state (for instance, the mingled shock, sadness, and curiosity in the second verse-unit of Whitman's "A Sight in Camp in the Daybreak Gray and Dim") and its degree of intensity: the two axes of reference for the qualitative character of a passage or a whole poem.

The *lyrical structure* of a poem, it follows, is the overall strategy of movement—the progression, juxtaposition, and interrelation of all the lyric centers, dynamic shifts, and minor tonal notes that make up the work. (A *tonal note* is the emotional or sensuous coloration of a phrase, line, sentence, or other small unit of a larger passage. Typically, a lyric center derives its depth, richness, and body from a combination of such notes.) Closely related to the lyrical structure is the poem's *dynamics:* in a large sense its rhythm of feeling, where "feeling" connotes all aspects of emotionally and sensuously charged awareness. More technically, the dynamics of the poem reside in the shifts of feeling and intensity among its separate lyric or affective or tonal units. These shifts may be gentle *modulations* or, at the furthest extreme, wrenching turns of emphasis or focus or emotional pitch *(torques)*. The varied pattern of these shiftings constitutes the overall dynamics of a poem.

A more elusive yet essential aspect of poetic structure is the illusion, in the successive lyric centers of a poem, that they embody a unified series of zones or qualities of individual human consciousness and experience. We may call this changing semblance the poem's *float of sensibility*. It can take on radically different characteristics at different points along the way. (The intimate character, the strong sense we have of mental energies at work, make it convenient to refer to a "speaker" at times, but this usage is inaccurate except when the poem itself presents an identified speaker; even then, the succession of tones and perspectives may prove chameleonlike, for there is of course no real speaker in the poem—only balancings of units of language. A speaking character, or "voice," is one of many possible devices for affective coloration. Consistency of speaker or attitude is not the point, as every poem we have so far examined has shown.)

Something both subtler and more formative is pervasively present, however: the poem's *initial* (or *psychological*) *pressure*. This is the directive source of disturbance and response that has energized the poem's process of association, realization, and counterpressure—the human context within which it defines itself. Poems with an obviously autobiographical, narrative, or dramatic cast generally suggest a human occasion as the initial pressure that has brought them into being. More basically, however, any kind of intellectual or passionate or imaginative engagement—including the assimilation of earlier literary works and modes—can contribute to the initial pressure. It is important to remember, though, that the pressure spoken of here reveals itself in the specific language of the poem as one of its essential and active ingredients. External information is irrelevant in itself, although it may help us discern something important in the poem we might not otherwise have seen as quickly.

The direct relation of poetry to all the concerns of life and thought is a matter of *expression,* not argument. "It *will* flame out," as Gerard Manley Hopkins puts it in "God's Grandeur" (though without my italics and in reference not to poetry but to the presence of God). The implied sense of the whole of life, concentrated in a particular aesthetic formation of language, cannot be contrived rhetorically but reveals itself in every nuance of a poem's style and phrasing. Poems may project existential tangles and problems and even get an idiosyncratic fix on them; they're hardly likely to solve them for us, or teach us much beyond poor blinded Gloucester's open-ended bit of wisdom toward the end of *King Lear:* "And that's true too." Yet they do express everything more pointedly and unreservedly than rhetoric can ever hope to do—but selectively: one possible conformation in the chaos of awareness at a time. Let me give one final instance, Sylvia Plath's "Child":

> Your clear eye is the one absolutely beautiful thing.
> I want to fill it with color and ducks,
> The zoo of the new
>
> Whose names you meditate—
> April snowdrop, Indian pipe,
> Little
>
> Stalk without wrinkle,
> Pool in which images
> Should be grand and classical

Not this troublous
Wringing of hands, this dark
Ceiling without a star.

This is not a discourse on child-parent relationships, but it presents a helpless juxtaposition of loving sweetness and high hopes for the child with an imagery of stifled depression. The charming affection and protectiveness of the first tercet, the delight in words shared with the child in the second, the shift to admiring apostrophe in the third (with its overtones at the same time of unreachable ideals), and the anguish of the fourth present the dilemma of an intractably balked spirit.

The dynamics of the poem are such that it moves from an atmosphere of fanciful joy to the charm of a world of tiny, lovely precisions of naming flowers; then to a sense of failure to meet a natural psychological need (the child, whose "clear eye is the one absolutely beautiful thing," *should* be given "grand and classical images" to reflect in the "pool" of her vision); and at last to pure distress and an atmosphere of being entombed within blackness while still living, so that nothing colorful or gay or beautiful or grand— no "star"—is available to be reflected in the "pool" of the child's sensibility.

The affective growth of the poem from a happy state to its doomed and abject opposite is marked by a constantly deepened gravity of phrasing. From the beginning the shifts are foreshadowed, at first almost invisibly. (The child's eye is "the one absolutely beautiful thing" in a life presumably otherwise unbeautiful. We are told that "I want to fill it" with everything that it should see with pleasure— not that "I" am doing so. These implied reservations take on negative resonances only when the poem's reversal of feeling is clear—something true even of the "should be" near the end of the third tercet.) The helpless sense of having nothing but oppressive blackness and misery to be reflected in the clear pool of the child's mind makes all the lively, appealing early images resonate with the pathos of lost possibilities.

"Child" does not present a specific dramatic situation. It does not explicitly present itself as a mother addressing her child. Especially, it does not tell us what we know from other sources: that the poet was chronically suicidal and, at the point of writing this poem, on the verge of her final, successful attempt. Enough is implied by the language to suggest an intense relationship quickened by extreme attentiveness to sense-impressions and complexities of feeling. The poem's movement and patterned formation express a unified awareness that could never be broken down intelligibly by logical prose analysis. And part of the expression is the curious satisfaction gained by making a formal design in language out of the elements of psychological pressure that brought the poem into being. It is not an expression of breakdown but of realized, tormenting, contradictory awareness held beautifully in momentary stasis.

FIVE

Form: The Poem's Musical Body

*I*t *should not surprise us that* the most profoundly moving poetry is likely to be the most accomplished in its craft. These qualities must be reciprocal, simultaneous, and in fact well-nigh identical. The mere placement of stresses, pauses, sound-echoes and contrasts, and a broad range of other such effects is expressive in every possible way, from sheer mimicry to the subtlest resonances. Speech is after all physical, even when it utters abstractions or nuances of feeling; this fact is important to our sense that a poem comes to birth with something like an organic body.

In a famous passage in Shakespeare's *Macbeth* (at the start of Act I, Scene vii), we overhear Macbeth soliloquizing. He is readying himself to murder Duncan, his king, and take over power. But just when he needs to be resolute, he is full of religious and practical doubts:

> If it were done, when 'tis done, then 'twere well
> It were done quickly: if th'assassination
> Could trammel up the consequence, and catch,
> With his surcease, success; that but this blow
> Might be the be-all and the end-all....here,
> But here, upon this bank and shoal of time,
> We'ld jump the life to come.

Macbeth reminds himself, too, of the obvious moral objections to the crime: his honor as a host, his loyalty to Duncan both as kinsman and as subject, and Duncan's blameless character. He seems shocked by his own thoughts:

>   Besides, this Duncan
> Hath borne his faculties so meek, hath been
> So clear in his great office, that his virtues
> Will plead like angels, trumpet-tongued, against
> The deep damnation of his taking-off:
> And pity, like a naked new-born babe,
> Striding the blast, or Heaven's cherubin, horsed
> Upon the sightless couriers of the air,
> Shall blow the horrid deed in every eye,
> That tears shall drown the wind. I have no spur
> To prick the sides of my intent, but only
> Vaulting ambition, which o'erleaps itself,
> And falls on th'other—

The first of these two passages starts in a nervous rush and races toward the word "quickly," expressing the urgency with which Macbeth must act if he is to succeed. Its thirteen successive opening monosyllables are restlessly emphatic and, at the same time, furtive—as if his very thoughts might be overheard. The repeated pronoun "it" sounds evasively noncommittal, while at the same time the repeated verb "done" hammers at the desired action toward which he is being impelled. The two caesuras fragmenting the first line, and all the tiny clauses making up much of the first sentence (with their wealth of varied grammatical parallelism and of internal rhymes and half-rhymes), add to the effect of anxious, whispering self-coaching. So does the repetition of "were," which fixes the whole state of mind of the passage by starting it off in the conditional mood. The meter, too, reinforces the uneasy mixture of haste, unsureness, and forced purposefulness:

> If it were dóne, when 'tís done, thén 'twere wéll
> It wére done quíckly . . .

One should not be dogmatic about stress-pattern, especially with verse so alive and open to varied orchestration. The initial torsion and hurried speculation are the main thing. As I have just scanned the opening, it strays from perfectly regular blank verse only in its stress on the first syllable, "If," in preparation for the repeated conditional "were." It is notable that, although "were" and "done" both recur three times, each is placed but once in stress-position; also, despite the internal rhyme of "when" and "then," only the latter is stressed. So there is repetition without monotony, and a sort of off-center balance that matches the speaker's disturbed and excited thought. A complex state of feeling is reinforced by the rhythm; an actor might choose among possible emphases at almost every turn to highlight this or that nuance.

The conditional mood holds throughout this first passage: a long sentence that is a pipe dream of murder without retribution in this life at least. That murderers cannot hope for redemption in "the life to come" is taken for granted. But the suggestion of willingness to forgo ("jump") eternal life in exchange for eluding punishment before death is so bold it needs to be masked both grammatically and metaphorically. Even so, it brands Macbeth with the mark of Cain.

I have quoted only the opening and closing of his soliloquy, to suggest how far the whole speech moves. The second passage swings into an entirely new realm of feeling, eulogizing Duncan and imagining, with inspired empathy, how decent people would regard his assassination. The effect is to leave the speaker exposed, by his own language, as a creature driven by paltry, pointless motives.

The reorientation of perspective here is largely a matter of the musical management of language. The phrasal units between pauses in the second passage are, on the whole, longer and more richly packed with feeling than those in the first. I shall note just three clear examples, each of which sustains an unbroken soaring movement from one line to the next: "that his virtues / Will plead like angels," "against / The deep damnation of his taking-off," and "horsed / Upon the sightless couriers of the air." The rhythmic method contributes mightily to the impact of the imagery in each instance. By contrast, the final line—returning attention to Macbeth's meanness of spirit—is cut off abruptly with the weak, anticlimactic phrase "And falls on th'other."

The life of a work of art is inseparable from the "technical" aspects of its form, such as we have just been observing. Far from being only incidental, qualities of sound and rhythm give a poetic work its organic body. Take away the specific patterns of verbal harmony and dissonance, or of speeding up or slowing down the pace, or of the weighting of pauses, and you reduce a dance of feeling to lumbering, obscure verbosity. Thus, an earnest series of books called

"Shakespeare Made Easy," designed for high school students, prints a "full modern translation" in prose alongside each page of Shakespeare's texts. The laudable purpose is to make sure students grasp the meaning of what they have been told to read. But do the following prose versions, placed opposite the passages under discussion, carry out that purpose?

> If we could get away with the deed after it's done, then the quicker it were done, the better. If the murder had no consequences, and his death ensured success . . . If, when I strike the blow, that would be the end of it— here, right here, on this side of eternity—we'd willingly chance the life to come.

and:

> Besides, this Duncan has used his power so gently, he's been so incorruptible in his great office, that his virtues will plead like angels, their tongues trumpeting the damnable horror of his murder. And pity, like a naked newborn babe or Heaven's avenging angel riding the winds, will cry the deed to everyone so that tears will blind the eye. I've nothing to spur me on but high-leaping ambition, which can often bring about one's downfall.

These are intelligent enough paraphrases, yet they illustrate the inadequacy of paraphrase in conveying the *sense* of poetry, let alone its artistry. Even at the level of literal meaning, the rush of insight into the doomed character of the intended action—an action held suspended in a moment of full clarity but not abandoned—has lost its paradoxical conviction. And what has happened to the "sightless couriers"? How did "blow the horrid deed in every eye, / That tears shall drown the wind" come to mean "cry the deed to everyone so that tears blind the eye"? Finally, how does the deliberately incomplete, faltering, and self-depreciative "o'erleaps itself, / And falls on th'other" become the tamely pat "can often bring about one's downfall"?

No. Such poetry requires reading and listening, not "translating" into some lesser thing. Far better to encourage students to say the verse aloud, hearing how it sounds and discussing what they hear, with the help of a teacher who, one hopes, is prepared and responsive to its values. I do not intend a diatribe against a perfectly honest effort. But the effort shows the innate impossibility of "getting" a poem's meaning by changing its character. (Asking students to try paraphrase for purposes of discussion may be useful, but doing it *for* them is fatal.) In any case, once we turn away from the artist's work in its own form and idiom, there is really nothing left to be experienced. The art itself, the pleasure and the struggles toward realization in it, is the whole point.

On the other hand, active translation from one language into another is a different matter entirely. Here the process demands alert attention to the precise art of the original. The effort to catch hold of its idiosyncratic quality—to catch it alive—is impossible, we must admit. The life of a poem consists in its gathering and transformations of sound, emotionally fusing individual feeling with the secret workings of the overtones of language. Yet the

attempt to evoke the affective character of the original can
be irresistible when a poem begins to haunt one's ear.

I have had this impulse from time to time (as one or
two translations in earlier chapters have already shown)—
most recently in response to a brief, beautiful poem in
Catalan by J. V. Foix: *"Es feia fosc i miravem l'estesa de pells a
cal baster"* ("It Was Growing Dark and We Stared at the
Hides Scattered about the Saddler's House"). This poem
presents itself as a sequence of events but actually unfolds
into a collage or, more actively, a montage of images. But
to say this hardly suggests its reach of association.

> Ja els fumerols acotxen els jardins;
> Les rels, per terra i murs, s'ajoquen al misteri.
> Tots dos, efígies de cuir abandonades
> A la fosca arenella de la nit,
> Cedim, fraterns, a l'hora fraudulosa.
> Abrivades, les egües, afolcades,
> Nades a l'ombra i a l'ombra nodrides,
> Assolen els poblats.
> Damunt la pell d'elefant del cel
> Els astres obren llurs camins airosos.
>
> [Already vapors enfold the gardens;
> Roots draw back into mystery, in earth and in
>   walls—
> All the mock skins of things, now forgotten,
> Lost in the deep sandpits of the night.
> Friendly, we cede them to the deceitful hour.
> Aroused and nervous, herds of mares,
> Born in shadow and nourished in shadow,
> Reach the tiny hamlets.
> High above the elephant pelt of the sky
> The stars open out their airy pathways.]

Few poems could better illustrate the affinity of poetic with musical form: the reaching out in both for felt mysteries forever elusive. This poem exists in a kind of nervous ecstasy of balances, between *"Ja els fumerols acotxen els jardins"* (the mistily changing scene down below on earth) and *"Els astres obren llurs camins airosos"* (the vast streams of starlight far up above the clouds). Its successive barely related metaphors, each comprising three lines at most, make their momentary appearances between these parallel yet opposite opening and closing images. Although they seem independent of one another, the pressure of association among the several metaphors nevertheless dominates the poem. They accompany the sense, at once enchanted and foreboding, of the ever-encroaching night.

Also, the metaphors are elements of a proliferating imagery of skins (or coverings, or contexts, or concealments, or even things merely connected with leather). Everything is an illusion or pelt of something else—so much so that perhaps the "saddler's house" of the title is simply the wide world with its endless nexus of secrets within secrets: the only "revelation" we're ever likely to get, though less harshly thrust at us here than in certain other poems of Foix's. One by one, we are told, we "cede" the familiar appearances of things, themselves deceptive *"efígies de cuir abandonades"* ("mock skins of things, now forgotten"—or more literally, "leather effigies, abandoned"), in exchange for other mock appearances. "The deceitful hour" *("l'hora fraudulosa")* of changing forms finds us friendly and receptive *("fraterns")* to its trickery. And no wonder, given the lovely images of the darkening world as herds of mares galloping toward all the tiny hamlets, and of the clear open pathways of light the stars create above the "elephant pelt of the sky," that end the poem.

The charm of these images may make us forget, for a moment, that they are figments of a "deceitful hour" of a type to which the human mind is all too amenable. It is, indeed, a kind of conspiracy between ever-changing outward forms in nature and our subjective natures. Negative notes (such as *"efígies"* and *"abandonades"* and *"fraudulosa"*) dot the poem in the midst of its exquisite play of sound, rhythm, and visual impressions. The assonance, consonance, and internal rhymes alone (to say nothing of the gardens disappearing in shrouds of mist, the shadow-mares, or the gracious stars) could seduce an angel into losing sight of the implied malaise and insecurity.

Every element of sound-design that has to be sacrificed in translation—at least until some unexpected breath of ingenuity allows its approximate duplication—causes a pang and heightens the translator's sense of the quality of the original. If you let your eye run down the left of Foix's Catalan lines, for instance, you can see that the second syllables *("els"* and *"rels,"* and then *"dos"* and *"fos-")* of each of the first two pairs of lines rhyme. Also, an alliterative pattern of *f*'s threads through most of the poem, connecting many important words: *"fumerols," "efígies," "fosca," "fraterns," "fraudulosa," "afolcades,"* and *"elefant";* and the liquid streams of *r* and *l*'s cause an almost subliminal savoring of successive phrases. These lingering echoes attach themselves to Foix's tones of mingled mystery, frustration, sadness, and entrancement. Foix seems to exult simultaneously in a feeling of transcendent delight and in the depressed sense that all is deception. The repeated sounds connecting his key phrases help blend exalted transport with its disillusioned opposite.

Such elements, like the irregular meter of the lines (which, however, *tend,* except in line 8, to have four or five stresses), cannot be exactly duplicated without the poem's becoming a grostesque parody. The translator must convey, first of all, the emotional and rhythmic timbre of the original in idiomatic, unforced language that gets as close to its moment-by-moment diction and movement as possible. Thus, I have tried to provide echoings and varied weights of lines and pauses similar to those of my model, whenever the differences between English and Catalan makes them feasible. Alliteration of *s*'s replaces Foix's *f*'s to some extent (as in the fifth line, but elsewhere too), and the liquids play a role similar to his. The original remains *the* poem of reference, of course, but the charm and terror implicit in its metamorphic vision has its reflections, if nothing more, in the translation.

The mechanical rendering of a poem—i.e., a literal word-for-word translation, forced into an approximation of the original verse-pattern—is, like prose paraphrase, only minimally useful and always a kind of betrayal.[1] The art of translation is a matter of connecting sensuously and idiomatically with the life and form of the original: a loving and admittedly risky enterprise for even the most gifted poet.

In the broadest sense, what I have been discussing in this chapter is *prosody,* a term defined in the *Princeton Ency-*

---

[1] See Stanley Burnshaw, *The Poem Itself* (New York: Holt, Rinehart and Winston, 1960) for a most valuable discussion, with many examples, of the translator's task.

clopedia of Poetry and Poetics (by far the most useful reference work on its subjects) as "the elements and structures
involved in the rhythmic or dynamic aspect of speech . . .
or in the compositions of the literary arts." The study of
prosody is usually confined to metrical analysis, but in a
somewhat freer sense it includes sound-values of all sorts
as they function in a poem. The *Princeton Encyclopedia* and
other studies and handbooks present basic considerations
of prosody—matters of theory, systems of scansion, historical aspects—in valuable detail, and a reader seeking systematic information concerning these considerations will
be enriched by going to such sources. However dry and
unimpassioned they often appear, they do deal with vital
matters. Poets over the centuries, including our contemporaries, have sometimes waged fierce battle over questions of prosody: witness Milton's attack on the use of rhyme
in poetry of heroic scope; or the efforts of Wordsworth
and Coleridge to adapt conventional verse to natural, idiomatic speech; or Whitman's replacement of such verse in
his own writing by a "free" pattern based mainly on the
incantatory, parallel rhythms of Biblical models and of vivid
oratory, sermons, and epic catalogues; or the "free verse"
experiments of our own century, taking many turns right
down to our own moment. These efforts and struggles,
and many others, have accompanied the dual task of
adapting poetic form to new pressures and permutations
of sensibility while maintaining a rigorous watch against
descent into self-indulgence, formlessness, and mere
slackness.

   Unlike linguists and scientific prosodists, poets have
generally not, however, been "objective" students of prosody. With every sort of individual variation, they have grown

into poetry (their own and that of others) through being
in love with language and through gradual absorption of
what they read and hear. Whether poets or not, though, I
am reasonably sure that most people who respond to poetry
have come to do so in the same way (aided by school experience, if they are extremely lucky). The prosody, together
with the rest of the physical body, of a poem (the successive units of phrasing and imagery, as in Foix's *"Es feia
fosc . . ."*), insinuates its patterns and connections by unpre-
dictable degrees.

This fact was brought home to me recently when I had
occasion to try to reach back to what it was in T. S. Eliot's
art that had so attracted some of my friends and me in
high-school days, a few years before his "Burnt Norton"
appeared in 1936. Leafing through his earlier pieces, I came
upon "The *Boston Evening Transcript*," a pre-1920s satirical
squib enlivened by an opening that is still visually hilar-
ious: "The readers of the *Boston Evening Transcript* / Sway
in the wind like a field of ripe corn."

We were living in Boston when I first read that poem,
and so knew the *Transcript*. With its marvelously leisurely
front page, full of white space, and its understated title, it
was so sedate! Eliot's first two lines were like an animated
cartoon; after them a subtler tone insinuated itself.

> When evening quickens faintly in the street,
> Wakening the appetites of life in some
> And to others bringing the *Boston Evening
>   Transcript,*
> I mount the steps and ring the bell, turning
> Wearily, as one would turn to nod good-bye to La
>   Rochefoucauld,
> If the street were time and he at the end of the
>   street,

> And I say, "Cousin Harriet, here is the *Boston Evening Transcript.*"

A phrasing like "evening quickens faintly in the street," quintessential early Eliot at his best, has nothing sensational about it, but it will slip into the memory almost without one's noticing. It is serious, precise, mysterious. And the subtle resonances around it (the internal off-rhyming of "evening" and all the participles, for instance; or the echoed *k*'s, *n*'s, and short *i*'s in *"Transcript,"* "quickens," and "wakening") are only a few examples of the poem's virtuosity, most impressive to young poets-in-the-making who spoke it aloud. Our young ears were ravished by the strategically distributed consonance and assonance and repetition (as in the Foix poem) and the remarkably varied series of five-stress lines—stretched to seven stresses in the antepenultimate and final lines—which exquisitely act out the bored self-distancing affected at the end. Needless to say, we spent precious little time analyzing the prosody in this fashion; nevertheless, we were responding to it more or less unconsciously. The way it gave the little poem more dimensions than seemed probable—dimensions of wit and irreverence and atmospheric accuracy—was something to be absorbed first and objectified at leisure.

The process of absorption of this sort begins long before adolescence, however, and is hardly limited to future poets—or perhaps it would be truer to say it is a natural aspect of our human need for, and love of, language. The beginning of James Joyce's *A Portrait of the Artist as a Young Man* takes us back to a child's earliest memories, which seem here to coincide with his response to language just as he is emerging from babyhood. (He is at once typical and especially sensitive.)

Once upon a time and a very good time it was there was a moocow coming down along the road and this moocow that was coming down along the road met a nicens little boy named baby tuckoo. . . .

His father told him that story: his father looked at him through a glass: he had a hairy face.

He was baby tuckoo. The moocow came down the road where Betty Byrne lived: she sold lemon platt.

O, the wild rose blossoms
On the little green place.

He sang that song. That was his song.

O, the green wothe botheth.

When you wet the bed first it is warm then it gets cold. His mother put on the oilsheet. That had the queer smell.

His mother had a nicer smell than his father. She played on the piano the sailor's hornpipe for him to dance. He danced:

Tralala lala
Tralala tralaladdy
Tralala lala
Tralala lala.

This opening passage harks back to the first glimmerings of poetic sensibility, rooted in a mixture of sensuous perception, delight in repeated words and rhythms, and the loving rituals of parental attention. Also, it recalls a young child's intent need to identify objects and experiences. ("His father told him that story . . ." "He sang that song. That was his song." "When you wet the bed first it is warm then it gets cold. His mother put on the oilsheet. That had the queer smell.") The remembered baby talk is a mixture of infant speech and adult cooing ("nicens," "baby tuckoo," "O, the green wothe botheth"), and is in turn mingled with the grown-up diction of the first snatch of song and of a sentence like "She played on the piano the sailor's hornpipe for him to dance." For in fact what we have in this passage is not a child's stream of consciousness—not purely that, at any rate—but a selective repossession of it through a filter of time.

The repossession is of a psychic state similar to that of most children born into the same culture. But the selective process of presentation is such that it stresses the potentially poetic sensibility of the child through the overwhelming emphasis on the early impact of language in various design formations: the non-stop, highly repetitious and internally rhyming first paragraph, for instance; and the parallel shorter sentences and clauses; and varied bits of song-lyrics. Strong sense-impressions are incorporated into the structure of the passage. The point is that the child not only has them but objectifies them verbally: the father's "hairy face," the precise sensations accompanying wetting the bed, particular smells. And the movement of this little body of prose—as is customary in Joyce's writing—is fundamentally that of a poem. Each of the small paragraphs is a carefully balanced unit of prose-poetry that parallels the others in brevity and introduces a new focus of attention preoccupying the child's absorbed attention. Meanwhile, the lyrical snatches not only call attention to their own magnetic appeal for him but also heighten our realization that we are reading a kind of concentrated free verse. (Indeed, anyone looking at Eliot's *The Waste Land,* which is comparably interspersed with such lyrical snatches, may infer a probable influence by Joyce, whose book appeared in 1916, six years before Eliot's poem.)

Joyce's opening passage reveals a good deal. It beautifully illustrates the fact that the organic body of a piece of writing—whether its form be one of the more familiar verse-modes or that of poetic prose—depends for its convincingness on the "technique" that goes into its making. The word "technique," often preceded by "mere" when used by people without a sense of what the *art* of poetry entails, does have a mechanical ring to it. But from the point of view of the poet—who as a working craftsman knows that an honest piece of labor is never "merely" anything—even "mechanical" is not such a deadly word after all. The resources of language are the poet's plastic materials, as various sorts of stone, clay, and bronze are the sculptor's; and the poet's knowledge of prosodic possibilities and traditions would roughly correspond to the sculptor's tools and his training in using them. A "feeling" for the materials and tools, in relation to the function of what is being made, is the mark of a master in either art. I've no doubt this analogy is oversimplified, but it is a very useful starting point (as opposed to abstract definitions of poetry not anchored in poetic practice) for seeing what technique actually accomplishes.

Returning to the Joyce passage, we can see how carefully its kinds and levels of language have been chosen and arranged. These are the artist's materials: adult baby talk; child-speech; short sentences projecting the tot's innocent pondering, yet grammatically perfect; a run-on sentence evoking his unselfconscious sensations; lyrical notes from the storehouse of popular song; and plain language of aesthetic discrimination ("the queer smell," "a nicer smell"). Joyce divides his materials into small segments and orders them cumulatively, but with a good deal of internal shifting of tonalities. He is clearly adapting essential lyric structure to prose-fiction. The small paragraphs and patches of song correspond to the separate verse-units of a poem. The varied parallelisms, strategically placed, of longer sentences, runs of shorter, choppy ones, and bursts of singing provide the kind of dynamics—successive affective impacts with a minimum of overt transition and authorial comment—that we associate with modern lyric poetry. A nostalgic atmosphere is set up, for example, at the very start, through the traditional language of storytellers: "Once upon a time . . ." It has a certain timbre we connect with legendry. But that tone is dropped almost at once, having as it were set the stage of childhood-recovery, as the passage goes on to ring its many changes.

All this strategy is certainly the result of technique: a skilled craftsman's use of his tools. At the same time (to grasp another handle of the endlessly fascinating problem of the formation of poems), there is an unknown in the matter. The power of expression, like the prior gift of empathy with reality outside oneself, can be strengthened by training but not created by it. We can appreciate the achievement of craftsmanship, and the writer can extend his mastery by attentive analysis; and yet work that reaches a certain pitch cannot easily be separated into imagination or inspiration on the one hand and technical virtuosity on the other. An irreversible fusion has taken place. We have witnessed the emergence of organic expression, having to do with the child's absorption of what his immediate existential world feeds into him. Let me quote just a few more

sentences that continue the passage, to suggest the widen-
ing orbit of Stephen's awareness. We have seen him danc-
ing to the simple refrain *"Tralala lala."* And then:

> Uncle Charles and Dante clapped. They
> were older than his father and mother but
> uncle Charles was older than Dante.
> Dante had two brushes in her press. The
> brush with the maroon velvet back was for
> Michael Davitt and the brush with the green
> velvet back was for Parnell. Dante gave him
> a cachou every time he brought her a piece
> of tissue paper.

At this point the child knows nothing about Dante
Alighieri as yet, or about Irish politics, but his vocabulary
has been broadened to include reference to them. We are
not told just who "Dante"—later called "Mrs. Reardon"—
is. (The character is based on Joyce's governess, also called
"Dante"—a curious nickname.[2]) And the two famed Irish
names are for the child only personifications of the brushes.
(Nor would he associate the green color "for Parnell" with
the symbolic shamrock.) So a body of future engagement
is surrounding him. The germ of his coming struggle with
his upbringing has been implanted in the book very early
on, as an element of the growth of an innocent soul.

I am stressing the work of Joyce for the moment because
the entire body of his fiction is a mobilization of prose forms
by lyrical method. All valued fiction has its important
dimension of lyrical structure: its dependence on intensely
realized moments presented in evocative, highly rhythmi-

---

[2] See Richard Ellmann, *James Joyce* (New York: Oxford University Press, 1982),
p. 25.

cal language that approaches pure poetry as we ordinarily think of it. Examples—from Tolstoy, Chekhov, Dostoevsky, Flaubert, Mark Twain (specifically, certain parts of *The Adventures of Huckleberry Finn*), Melville, Hemingway, Faulkner, and many others—flood the mind. But it was Joyce who made lyrical structure primary in his writing. The germ of political engagement implanted in the paragraph on Dante's two brushes explodes a short while later in the fiery quarrel during Christmas dinner. The language of passionate adult partisanship (Parnellites versus adherents of the Church's position) flares up in vividly rhythmic clashing statements, interspersed with equally rhythmic conflict between deliberately coarse male language of insult and genteel language of feminine indignation. Joyce handles each of his larger units as a developing poetic structure, and leads us, without transitions, to balance them against one another as we would segments of a poetic sequence. The shock of the passage just described is enormously heightened because it intrudes so violently on a child's uncomprehending—but rapidly assimilating—mind.

But to return to our first emphasis: the affective power of this shock is highly dependent on the author's ear for excited, genuine speech:

> [Mr Casey] threw his fist on the table and, frowning angrily, protruded one finger after another.
> —Didn't the bishops of Ireland betray us in the time of the union when bishop Lanigan presented an address of loyalty to the Marquess Cornwallis? Didn't the bishops and priests sell the aspirations of their country in

1829 in return for catholic emancipation?
Didn't they denounce the fenian movement
from the pulpit and in the confessionbox?
And didn't they dishonour the ashes of Terence Bellew MacManus?

His face was glowing with anger and Stephen felt the glow rise to his own cheek as
the spoken words thrilled him. . . .

—God and religion before everything!
Dante cried. God and religion before the
world!

Mr Casey raised his clenched fist and
brought it down on the table with a crash.

—Very well, then, he shouted hoarsely, if
it comes to that, no God for Ireland!

—John! John! cried Mr Dedalus, seizing
his guest by the coatsleeve.

At the same time, we can discern the deliberate patterning here. Among its more obvious elements, we may
note the alternation of one-sentence paragraphs of narration and description with paragraphs that present speech
(a pattern slightly altered at the end). The first three action-
sentences all use the conjunction "and"; also, the third re-
peats many words and phrases of the first. The longest of
the paragraphs, Mr. Casey's excoriation of the bishops and
priests, is a series of parallel rhetorical sentences. Indeed,
the passage is thick with repetition and parallelism of several sorts, including occasionally heavy alliteration (e.g., the
f's in the first sentence) and some internal rhyme (e.g.,
"address" and "Marquess," "aspirations" and "emancipation," and such off-rhymes as "Stephen" and "religion,"
"union" and "fenian," and "denounce" and "Terence").

I first mentioned *A Portrait of the Artist as a Young Man*

to illustrate the importance of the prosodic element in conveying both the subjective states and the organic unfolding of feeling and awareness that are the special domain of poetry. Joyce's presentation of the growth into maturity of an artist-in-words had perforce to draw on and deploy the resources of lyrical technique to the limits of his ability. He had the double task of showing his protagonist absorbing those resources through all his senses (his ear especially) and of projecting his development through the structure and the constantly improvised minutiae of technique of the novel. The revolutionary intimacy and social awakening evoked in the book are inseparable from that structure and technique: a triumph of prose-poetry surpassed only in Joyce's next book: *Ulysses*.

The poet's absorption of the world wherein he dwells is highly mimetic. It means internalizing an experience or a way of talking or responding (Mr. Casey's speech and table-pounding, for instance; but also the deceptive appearances of objects as night descends in Foix's poem; or the self-contradictions of the secret mind as it prepares to carry out its momentous and frightful decision in *Macbeth*). In mimicking this internalization, a poem acts it out in language, with everything in its formal character participating in the effort. W. H. Auden's "On This Island" is virtually a memo to himself on how this happens:

> Look, stranger, on this island now
> The leaping light for your delight discovers,
> Stand stable here
> And silent be,
> That through the channels of the ear
> May wander like a river
> The swaying sound of the sea.

Here at the small field's ending pause
When the chalk wall falls to the foam and its tall ledges
Oppose the pluck
And knock of the tide,
And the shingle scrambles after the suck-
-ing surf,
And the gull lodges
A moment on its sheer side.

Far off like floating seeds the ships
Diverge on urgent voluntary errands,
And the full view
Indeed may enter
And move in memory as now these clouds do,
That pass the harbour mirror
And all the summer through the water saunter.

The poem is a prescription for absorbing into oneself
a particular scene and moment as through the eyes and
ears of a stranger—so that everything is felt keenly in its
own right. Each stanza begins with long lines locating the
range of vision, followed by two pivotal two-stress lines and
then lines of alternating greater and shorter length: a
graceful pattern for shifting perspectives held together by
a music of self-enchantment and symbolic musing. The
purest imagery of internalization comes, appropriately, in
the first stanza, especially in its final three lines, where the
ear is not only an instrument of "the swaying sound of the
sea" but conforms to it as though the inner self were its
natural channel. The winding pattern of line-lengths and
of delayed rhymes reinforces this imagery of internalized
sense-response that "wanders" through us and possesses
us. The feeling of giving oneself to complete empathy with
the external scene in all its active detail is deepened in the
slightly compressed final stanza, in which memory is seen

as the reflector and preserver of the desired sense of fresh immediacy. The ships bent "on urgent voluntary errands" are part of the immediate purview as well, but a vast extension of reference is now implied: a suggestion of the world's interdependency, of the germination ("like floating seeds") of new conditions through action, and of the equal reality of existence beyond the horizon. The slow, qualified affirmation in the third stanza's middle lines is given weight by the richer images in the long closing lines, but also made less portentous by the extremely leisurely ending, with its five stresses and its relaxed language: "And all the summer through the water saunter."

"On This Island" is the gentlest of the poems and passages cited in this chapter. It is quietly thoughtful and melodic at the same time, and yet it is as memorable as most poems with far greater overt intensity. For it embodies, with amazing simplicity, the very process of the poet's becoming an instrument of what he or she observes and absorbs—while at the same time the *poem* takes on a shape of its own, full of empathy with whatever has generated it but not limited by that source. The active patterning that evolves in the course of all this is an expressive force in itself, the means by which the poem discovers its driving emotions and creates a momentary equilibrium among them.

SIX

"Rigor of Beauty": Poetic Evaluation

I hope that everything said in preceding chapters has pointed to the sense of poetry as expression, not discourse. It is vital to bear the difference in mind, for poems very often engage with serious or "controversial" matters. Attitudes towards love, religion, and problems of every sort must, obviously, be charged with tension and passion, and poets are most certainly persons with opinions—creatures of their historical moments.

Examples abound. One has only to think of Yeats's pronouncements on eugenics, or his attraction at one time to William Morris's brand of aesthetic socialism and at another to an Irish fascist movement. Or one can recall Pound's and Eliot's observations on culture and anti-semitic forays (Pound's the more virulent, of course). Hugh MacDiarmid (Christopher Grieve) was simultaneously a Communist and a Scottish Nationalist. When an American customs official asked him if he had anything to declare, he answered "Aye, I'm verra Left!" Edwin Muir was a Social-

ist. All very true, and in its own context genuinely important. And yet . . .

And yet, nevertheless, a work of art transforms all that
generates or enters it. It absorbs, without obliterating, its
elements into a plastic structure not reducible to the artist's
stated motives and meanings. Its medium, which in literature is perforce language with all its permutations of sound
and association, will have its own history and resonances
beyond the individual artist's full knowledge. The greater
the work, the farther it carries beyond its creator's conscious horizons. Great adventure, great risk. The absorbing, never completely soluble subject of "greatness," and
of poetic *quality* and how we gauge it, has to do with
expressive power that the poet taps without quite controlling.

A classic instance is the *Divine Comedy*. This masterpiece
cannot be accounted for by Dante's narrow politics or his
wide theology, yet it does reveal the living subjective qualities of both for him. It projects every possible degree of
feeling, from intense melancholy through revulsion and
horror to elated liberation and rapturous harmony. The
Inferno itself, the first of the poem's three large divisions,
begins in darkness (a prelude to the descent into Hell) and
ends with escape into light again:

> Nel mezzo del cammin di nostra vita
>   mi ritrovai per una selva oscura
>   che la diritta via era smarrita.
> Ah quanto a dir qual era è cosa dura
>   esta selva selvaggia e aspra e forte
>   che nel pensier rinova la paura!
> Tant' è amara che poco è piu morte . . .

[At the midpoint of our life's journey
  I found myself lost in a dark forest
  with no clear path I could see anywhere.
Ah, how very hard it is even to name
  that forest, so dreadful and dense and wild
  that just mentioning it brings back all my terror!
So bitter it is that death is hardly worse.]

and:

Lo duca e io per quel cammino ascoso
  intrammo a ritornar nel chiaro mondo;
  e sanza cura aver d'alcun riposo
salimmo su, el primo e io secondo,
  tanto ch' i' vidi delle cose belle
  che porta 'l ciel, per un pertugio tondo;
e quindi uscimmo a riveder le stelle.

[My guide* and I, on that hidden pathway,
  began our return toward the bright outer world,
  and without pausing to rest, not for a moment,
we climbed straight up, he first, I second,
  far enough to see, through a round opening,
  some of the lovely sights Heaven shows forth;
and soon we emerged and once more gazed at the
        stars.]

The *Divine Comedy* is far too complex a structure to be discussed at length here. But even these few lines, for which I have provided only some rough beginnings of a translation, will suggest its supreme artistry. One can glimpse in them the ever-varying continuity of its terza rima pattern (tercets with the interlinking rhymes *aba, bcb,* and so on), the intimate immediacy of phrasing, and the constantly modulated pacing of the hendecasyllabic lines. My trans-

*Vergil

lation is intended simply to connect with the timbre of Dante's verse without forcing the English into an alien straitjacket. It ignores both the end-rhymes and the subtly placed half-rhymes and makes no attempt to measure the lines in eleven-syllable units. (The English language lacks the rhyming opportunities afforded by the great number of Italian words ending in unstressed syllables with a final vowel. It also lacks the kind of elision between words that allows them to be run together, making for a certain combined melody and density of a different kind than the typical stress measurement of English verse affords.)

As a result, my translation—although it seeks to suggest Dante's rhythm without mimicking his meter—inevitably loses important dimensions of his poetic grace and authority. Inevitably, too, it loses the special richness that comes with an intricate texture of reciprocal and echoing sound formations. And in a larger sense, it loses much of the kind of value we might call poetic memory; for poetry, which always exists in a certain tradition, evokes whole states of realization discovered in the works that are its forerunners. The opportunities for felicitous rhyme in Italian, for instance, when seized upon by a master with Dante's psychological readiness and sensuous and emotional imagination, exist within a continuum of creation shared with earlier and later poets. As Aldo S. Bernardo notes, "Many and varied were the poems that Dante had composed prior to the *Divine Comedy,* and everywhere is the influence of his predecessors evident."[1] This was far from saying he was a slavish imitator. Rather, he drank in whatever of value came his way—not always intentionally, I am sure. A poet

---

[1] Alex Preminger *et al.*, eds., *Princeton Encyclopedia of Poetry and Poetics* (Princeton: Princeton University Press, 1974), p. 409.

using a certain technique or device is also using the tradition within which it arose, whether or not the poet is aware of that fact.

As I have noted, it would absorb too much space to pursue, in detail, the beautiful intricacies of Dante's poem. But there is one aspect of the subject we should push into a bit further. It is not peculiar to Dante's work; instead, it is an elusive yet crucial aspect of the formation of poems generally, especially poems approaching greatness.

I refer to the impersonality of form—something almost invisible and yet the chief reason that art is not merely self-expression or—worse—the ornamental laying out of ideas. No one, not even a rare genius like Dante, can claim to have invented the materials of which poems are formed, or the sense of the possibilities for form itself. Dante was the first European to write a systematic defense of the common tongue in serious poetry; but for centuries poets throughout the world had already been using the vernacular. Again, he invented terza rima as a prosodic embodiment of the Christian symbolism permeating the *Divine Comedy;* but verse-units made up of tercets already existed in Italian poetry. And for that matter, meter and sound-patterning had long been integral to poetry and subject to experiment.

The active pressure toward expression inherent in language and its long evolution is an impersonal context into which individual persons are born. So is the more specialized pressure to shape language, as a melodic, emotion-bearing substance, into works of art. Clearly, in these respects, language and the art it makes possible are like fated circumstances of nature: gravity, or the contours of landscapes, or day and night and the seasons, or the realities of biology. (This is true as well of the other arts and their sources and materials.)

We can react to these circumstances of nature and culture, and even affect or alter them, but whenever we do a certain tension and resistance come into play. We are dealing with the partially intractable, and with forces antedating our individual selves. The creative process is in essence more a collaboration—and struggle—with the unknown, in ourselves as well as in the workings of nature and history, than we generally realize. For this reason it can lead a poet to have insights that contradict the most cherished assumptions he or she usually entertains. The profoundly humane moments in the *Divine Comedy* are of this order. An example is the incident of Dante's being so overcome by the fate of the sinning lovers Paolo and Francesca that he faints away, unable to cope with the irreconcilable contradiction between profane passion (so close to his own feelings) and the stern punishment imposed by divine law.

Even the juxtapositions of sound in a short unit—such as the grimly vehement seventh line of the *Inferno: "Tant' è amara che poco è piu morte"*—can stop the poem in its tracks because of what has been exposed, in this instance a state of deeply repressed panic. The compression of the line is reinforced by the explosively alliterative *p*'s in words of opposed meaning (*"poco"* and *"piu"*: "little" and "more") and by the less obvious consonantal echoes in the one dread, unsoftened word *"morte"* of *"tant' è amara."* The line is a pang of sudden bitter discovery.

The perspective just presented is implicit in literary art of all times, but has taken on preeminent importance in our century because of the impact of modern lyric poetry's liberation from the need to argue or explain or tell a story.

Modernism is foreshadowed in literature of the past whenever the lyric spirit, absolutely true to subjective awareness
and to the ambiguous and provisional character of our
actual apperception, comes into its own. Recognition of the
impersonal side of form militates against imposed moral-
izing or sentimentality and enables writers to protect themselves against facile and willful self-indulgence. The pressure of ideological and political determinism has long been
the curse of human thought, always allied to the winning
or consolidation of power. But the lyrical is the wild card
in human communion as in literature, in its insistence on
tentative perception and intimate psychological accuracy.
Tone, rhythm, concreteness of image, and coloration and
intensity of phrasing are essential in making brilliantly
precise the shadings of complex awareness by which we
guide our lives. Impersonal in themselves, they perform
this labor only when unforced.

James Joyce, the most democratic sensibility among the
modern masters, who nevertheless influenced the politically reactionary Pound and Eliot more than did any of
their contemporaries, points very sharply toward the
triumph of lyrical over ideological perspective. *A Portrait
of the Artist as a Young Man* is an exemplar of this triumph,
presented—as I have already suggested in the preceding chapter—through lyrical centers of prose-poetry disguised as broken narrative. (And not only of *prose*-poetry.
A rough count shows some thirty-one pages containing
poems, snatches or single lines of poems and songs, and
prayers and bits of prose arranged as poetry.) The book's
large effort is to slough off enslavement to institutional-
ized religious, national, and family commitment and also
to conventional expectations of love and marriage. This

effort is not polemical but an urgent, unfolding growth into freedom by the sensibility moving through the pages. The exchanges between Stephen, the protagonist, and Davin, his fellow-student who embodies a profound and pure nationalist spirit, are but one instance of the book's drive to replace emotional enslavement by a seriously dedicated aesthetic reorientation. Davin's tale of a chance encounter with a peasant woman, as innocent in her way as he, is deeply stirring and reveals the roots Stephen must tear out of himself on his way to freedom. Davin has been shocked by Stephen's confidences, which no doubt were tinged with a youthful Baudelairean affectation. Stephen is therefore constrained to spell out his feelings:

> —The soul is born, he said vaguely, first in those moments I told you of. It has a slow and dark birth, more mysterious than the birth of the body. When the soul of a man is born in this country there are nets flung at it to hold it back from flight. You talk to me of nationality, language, religion. I shall try to fly by those nets.

The progression of *Ulysses* is a far richer triumph of this order. From the start, the work accentuates the young protagonist's superior sensibility. With quiet emphasis, this quality is revealed in his acid political comments, pointed yet evading set positions, and subtly contrasted with a series of anti-semitic jokes and utterances—most notably by Haines, from whom Stephen remains aloof, and by Mr. Deasy, who talks of "jew merchants . . . at their work of destruction" and is answered without taking Stephen's point:

—A merchant, Stephen said, is one who
buys cheap and sells dear, jew or gentile, is
he not?

—They sinned against the light, Mr Deasy
said gravely. And you can see the darkness in
their eyes. And that is why they are wanderers on the earth to this day.

This is the passage, full of whirling thought, in which
Stephen says, "History . . . is a nightmare from which I am
trying to awake." The text continues:

On the steps of the Paris Stock Exchange,
the goldskinned men quoting prices on their
gemmed fingers. Gabbles of geese. They
swarmed, loud, uncouth, about the temple,
their heads thickplotting under maladroit silk
hats. Not theirs: these clothes, this speech,
these gestures. Their full slow eyes belied the
words, the gestures eager and unoffending,
but knew the rancours massed about them and
knew their zeal was vain. A hoard heaped by
the roadside: plundered and passing on. Their
eyes knew the years of wandering and, patient,
knew the dishonours of their flesh.

In this paragraph on the imagined Stock Exchange
scene, Stephen's fantasy takes over. A changing vision of
"jews" emerges in reverie, moving from the Deasy stereo-
type to ever more empathy with the "goldskinned men."
The next section, ending Part I of the book, takes us onto
the beach with Stephen during his isolated, highly lyrical
reverie. We have been readied for the appearance of Leo-
pold Bloom, Stephen's Jewish co-protagonist, at the start

of Part II. Bloom is less cultivated but equally sensitive and introspective, and is perforce a carrier of international historical memories. The political and the aesthetic have been fused—and the Odyssean voyage of dangerous departures is fully under way, having been foreshadowed in the words "wanderers on the earth" and "Their eyes knew the years of wandering . . ."

A surprising instance of a similar fusion occurs in Yeats's "The People," in *The Wild Swans at Coole*. This poem undercuts any simple ideological reading based on Yeats's more backward pronouncements. Indeed, it undercuts its own initial postures of contempt for the mob and of yearning for aristocratic elegance. The poem begins in egoistic protest:

'What have I earned for all that work,' I said,
'For all that I have done at my own charge?
The daily spite of this unmannerly town,
Where who has served the most is most defamed,
The reputation of his lifetime lost
Between the night and morning. I might have lived,
And you know well how great the longing has been,
Where every day my footfall should have lit
In the green shadow of Ferrara wall;
Or climbed among the images of the past—
The unperturbed and courtly images . . .'

To all this, the unnamed woman called "my phoenix" replies that she has suffered far more from the people's ingratitude. "Yet never," she says, "have I, now nor any time, / Complained of the people." (This despite the greater bitterness of her description of mistreatment.) Although the poet has a ready, rational reply to her affirmation, he confesses, in the poem's final lines, the force and nobility of her words:

And yet, because my heart leaped at her words,
I was abashed, and now they come to mind
After nine years, I sink my head abashed.

The passionate immediacy of this poem, humble and powerful at the same time, struck me long ago. In his reply to the woman, the poet has observed that, because she has "not lived in thought but deed," she "can have the purity of a natural force"—as opposed to the "analytic" probings of his mind. Her certainty comes from the fact that she herself is a living metaphor, indistinguishable from the democratic, revolutionary staunchness she affirms. Her faith in the people is uncalculating, in sharp distinction to the attitude in the poet's opening outburst, in which Yeats slyly depreciates himself by using the language of the market-place: " 'What have I earned for all that work,' I said, / 'For all that I have done at my own charge?' " No wonder he is "abashed" by her unqualified magnanimity.

"The People," in fact, is one of the most original love poems one is likely to read. To repeat a word just used, it is a *revolutionary* love poem of possession not only by another being but also by what that being embodies. With exquisite strategy, Yeats placed it third in a tiny sequence of eight poems quietly imbedded in *The Wild Swans at Coole*. The sequence begins with the perfect six-line poem of persistent, ineradicable love called "Memory" (formally paralleled, with variations, in the equally memorable penultimate poem, "A Deep-sworn Vow"). It ends with "Presences," a half-nightmare poem of "that monstrous thing / Returned and yet unrequited love." That "The People" should emerge in such a setting, converting its love-preoccupation into a political one and reversing rhetorical expectations in the process, is one remarkable sign of art's volatile reciprocities. It is a poem of 1915 and a token of how, in the dangerous, challenging world in which the great modern masters dreamt and worked, they awoke to a special new sense of associative freedom closely allied to an epic burden.

I am speaking of a world of potentialities, experiments, explorations: the world in which the truest contemporary poets are, necessarily, still pursuing the psyche's hidden formations. As we saw earlier in thinking of Pound's "The Coming of War: Actaeon" and of his later use of the Actaeon figure as a self-condemnatory reflex, it is impossible for a poet to foresee whither that pursuit will lead. An equally interesting instance is Yeats's double sequence, "Meditations in Time of Civil War" and "Nineteen Hundred and Nineteen." Yeats responds to terrorist violence with utter pain and pity and outrage:

> a drunken soldiery
> Can leave the mother, murdered at her door,
> To crawl in her own blood, and go scot-free.

But he is forced, by the state of awareness into which the sequences carry him, to admit his powerlessness and submit to the collapse of his aristocratic delusions:

> I count those feathered balls of soot
> The moor-hen guides upon the stream,
> To silence the envy in my thought;
> And turn towards my chamber, caught
> In the cold snows of a dream.

Modern writers like Yeats, Pound, and Joyce could break away from the automatic imperatives with which they had grown up. They did so by being able, from time to time, to get directly in touch with that semiconscious inner realm

of uncritical, candid awareness where the psyche dwells.
Their struggle to reach that realm beneath the level of set
attitudes, and to create tentative poetic structures that could
hold the competing pressures in action there in balance, is
crucial in their art. Humanly, it is far more representative
than any rhetorical document could possibly be.

Neither a writer's literal "message" nor its supposed
correctness determines a work's quality. On the other hand,
they are not irrelevant—provided we understand that a
subjective and aesthetic transference is taking place: the
"music again and always!" of the "winged living thing" that
Verlaine means by poetry. As it happens, all the quotations
given so far in this chapter present gravely serious matters.
The *Inferno* passages have to do with sinking into a state of
damnation and at last being released from it. The passages
by Joyce have to do with the task of freeing one's psyche
from unquestioned allegiances (Joyce's language about the
"soul" and its "birth" and "flight" overlaps with that of
Verlaine's "Art Poétique"), with anti-semitism, and with the
Jews' condition of exile. The Yeats quotations concern the
poet's relationship to his people, the power of a loved and
selflessly idealistic woman, political terror and armed
struggle, and the poet's sense of historical impotence. These
are hardly inconsiderable questions. Few people, in fact,
realize how drastically our outstanding modern poetry has
wrestled with the complexity, the intractability, and the
existential difficulties of historical circumstance as they enter
our interior lives and emotional experience. The subjective and aesthetic transference to which I have referred is
not an evasion of issues but a discovery of their living character.

In order to make this discovery, a poem must reach a

certain pitch that has the quality of "magic," though not necessarily by means of overtly incantatory language. "Magic" in art *may* be an aura of delighted enchantment, as in the "Introduction" to William Blake's *Songs of Innocence:*

> Piping down the valleys wild
> Piping songs of pleasant glee
> On a cloud I saw a child.
> And he laughing said to me.
>
> Pipe a song about a Lamb;
> So I piped with merry chear,
> Piper pipe that song again—
> So I piped, he wept to hear.
>
> Drop thy pipe thy happy pipe
> Sing thy songs of happy chear,
> So I sung the same again
> While he wept with joy to hear
>
> Piper sit thee down and write
> In a book that all may read—
> So he vanish'd from my sight.
> And I pluck'd a hollow reed.
>
> And I made a rural pen,
> And I stain'd the water clear,
> And I wrote my happy songs
> Every child may joy to hear[2]

The whole urgency here is toward expressing innocent, miraculous gaiety. All the energetic repetition—especially in the ecstatic first two lines that begin with "Piping"

[2] The Blake texts are taken from David Erdman, ed., *The Complete Poetry and Prose of William Blake* (Berkeley and Los Angeles: University of California Press, 1982), *q.v.*, pp. 786 ff. for comment on the punctuation, etc., "as [Blake] printed it."

(a word echoed again and again in the first two stanzas) and the biblical-sounding lines beginning with "And"—has the force of incantation and revelation. The central feeling is a dizzy sense of bliss and of the imperious passion to share both it and the pathos inevitably suggested by the association of the word "Lamb" with the sacrifice of Jesus. Blake's "happy song" is a triumph of poetic magic in its brighter aspect over the lurking threat of a darker magic.

Something like a state of transport, not necessarily joyous, is what takes a poem beyond ordinary discourse. That state is reached through a poet's formal mastery, imagination, and articulate subjective awareness. It is, indeed, "revelatory," and can be defined only by its own character as unfolded in the poem. I have quoted and discussed the "Introduction" to *Songs of Innocence* because it so very clearly, in so short a space, epitomizes these conditions of poetry and illustrates how poetic form helps set up an atmosphere of pure reverie or fantasy. It has an unusually regular and dominating metrical pattern of seven-syllable trochaic catalectic lines, all scanning like the first one: "Píping doẃn the válleys wíld." This pattern helps compel emotionally heightened attention because each line begins and ends so emphatically. The rhyme scheme, too, is emphatic. The second and fourth lines always rhyme— calling special attention to themselves in the fourth stanza, since "read" and "reed" have exactly the same pronunciation (an instance of rime riche). In addition, the first and third lines rhyme in two of the stanzas. The fact that all the rhyming words are monosyllables makes the scheme all the more emphatic. The speed of the poem, whose original burst of energy makes it seem to come rushing into view like the piper himself, counteracts the heaviness of these effects. The successful struggle to create a sense of joy triumphant is much bound up, then, with the formal technique.

In sharp contrast is the magic of Blake's "Infant Sorrow," a poem in *Songs of Experience:*

> My mother groand! My father wept.
> Into the dangerous world I leapt:
> Helpless, naked, piping loud;
> Like a fiend hid in a cloud.
>
> Struggling in my fathers hands:
> Striving against my swadling bands:
> Bound and weary I thought best
> To sulk upon my mothers breast.

At first the form here seems even simpler than that of "Introduction." "Infant Sorrow" is shorter, just two quatrains made up of rhyming couplets; and each line has four stresses, although the falling rhythm here is less dominant than in "Piping down the valleys wild." There is violent energy in "Infant Sorrow" too, but it is slowed down by being compressed into the successive separate couplets. Despite its brevity, it is perhaps a more complex and ambiguous poem, for we may read it both as an act of verbal empathy with the newborn baby's imagined terror and as a gently comic piece of tender sympathy—a sort of miniature mock-heroic foray.

This bit of squirming, howling humanity is certainly much different from the child in the other poem. For one thing, its physical situation is presented realistically; its mother brings it forth in pain while its father weeps with pity. The baby struggles against being held and against being wrapped in swaddling clothes. At last, constricted and fatigued, it "sulks" and perhaps refuses when offered the mother's breast. But still, the little "helpless, naked" being must give up the unequal struggle.

But not all the language is realistic. The lines "Into the dangerous world I leapt" and "Like a fiend hid in a cloud" are extremely dramatic, and can be taken as realistic only in a psychological sense. Certainly, the drastic experience of birth may well feel like a "leap" from the secure womb into the unknown. And the infant's screaming resistance may make it feel demonically driven—as it would surely seem to its distraught parents!

It is these lines especially that introduce the suspicion of a subtle whimsy at work, observing the baby's *Sturm und Drang* with amused compassion. There is gentle irony, too, in the baby's saying it finally "thought best" to give up and just "sulk upon my mothers breast." Very likely all the tonalities—that is, of demonically charged fear, sympathetic realism, and lovingly understood comic histrionics—coalesce in these highly compressed, moving stanzas.

Because they are brief, have obviously incantatory elements and also supernatural imagery, and are—on the surface at least—simple and direct, we can see the working of poetic "magic" quite clearly in Blake's pieces. The main thing is that, in the subjective realm that is the ambience of art, all states of thought and all connotations of language coexist. So do all details of memory, both personal and historical—whether they be literal or created in the imagination. Moreover, all ongoing art forms evoke innumerable associations of earlier styles and preoccupations and modes of belief. The state of transport in poetry that I have mentioned is reached when the level of artistry is high enough for a confluence of all these potential energies to take over a poem and carry it beyond the poet's own empirical limits.

Thus, Dante is enabled to present, simultaneously, the landscape of vision, a complex of everyday human feeling and observation, and the stuff of nightmares and day-dreams. He does so "naturally," with forms derived from Provençal predecessors (such as the sirventes, with its com-bination of lyrical, narrative, and satirical elements) and from religious allegory and the language of courtly love—together with a host of other sources in common speech and folklore and Church observance. Subjectively, we may have implicit "knowledge" of much that lies beyond our normal ken, depending on our ability to absorb the reso-nances of language and tradition. In Dante's case, we are speaking of such ability at the level of genius. This is true as well, if perhaps to a lesser degree, of Joyce and Yeats—as we can see, for instance, in the passages of half-mystical reverie by the one, and of longing to live "among the images of the past" by the other, quoted earlier in this chapter.

Considerations such as the ones I have just been advancing inevitably affect the way we look at unfamiliar poetry. That is, we have certain expectations connected with the word "poetry" itself, such as that it will use language in a heightened or aroused form, that its rhythmic pattern-ing will be a significant element, and that in some way it will reach for a state of transport or magic—that is, of the most alert subjectivity. But these expectations must not be turned into strict rules about what is or is not permissible. As Whitman puts it in the introduction to his 1855 *Leaves of Grass,* "Of the traits of the brotherhood of savans [sic] musicians inventors and artists nothing is finer than silent defiance advancing from new free forms."

Whitman's words stand as a clear warning. Readers

should avoid easy dismissal simply because they cannot at first see how those "new free forms" make for a genuine poetry. The early critics of Wordsworth's *The Prelude* were generally blind to its continuities with Milton's blank verse and epic conception—as they almost had to be. Time was needed for people to immerse themselves in it, absorb its idiosyncratic flavor, and recognize its originality of method. Thereafter, it gradually became easier to discern the kind of reorientation that Wordsworth had brought about when adapting classical and Miltonic verse to his purpose. He placed himself, speaking as a poet and thoughtful person of his age, at the center of a work of heroic scope. Instead of Achilles and Odysseus and Aeneas and Adam and Jesus, Wordsworth's own probing sensibility moves through the pages, progressing emotionally from one evocative situation to the next, presenting itself in language that is dignified but far more confiding in a personal way than Homer's or Vergil's or Milton's epics.

A few lines from the opening of *The Prelude* (1850 edition) will at least partly illustrate these points:

> O there is blessing in this gentle breeze,
> A visitant that, while he fans my cheek,
> Doth seem half-conscious of the joy he brings
> From the green fields, and from yon azure sky.
> Whate'er his mission, the soft breeze can come
> To none more grateful than to me; escaped
> From the vast City, where I long have pined
> A discontented Sojourner—Now free,
> Free as a bird to settle where I will.
> What dwelling shall receive me? in what vale
> Shall be my harbour? underneath what grove
> Shall I take up my home? and what clear stream
> Shall with its murmur lull me into rest?
> The earth is all before me: with a heart

Joyous, nor scared at its own liberty,
I look about; and should the chosen guide
Be nothing better than a wandering cloud,
I cannot miss my way. I breathe again;
Trances of thought and mountings of the heart
Come fast upon me: it is shaken off,
That burthen of my own unnatural self,
The heavy weight of many a weary day
Not mine, and such as were not made for me.

The passage is very personal, speaking of the enormous psychic release of being able to live in rural surroundings after the discontentment and heavy depression of "the vast City, where I long have pined." One line especially contains a direct echo ("The earth is all before me") of the close of *Paradise Lost;* but the whole situation presented seems a sequel, recast in introspective, untheological terms, to that in the Milton passage:

In either hand the hast'ning Angel caught
Our ling'ring Parents, and to th'Eastern gate
Led them direct, and down the Cliff as fast
To the subjected Plain; then disappear'd.
They looking back, all th'Eastern side beheld
Of Paradise, so late their happy seat,
Wav'd over by that flaming Brand, the Gate
With dreadful Faces throng'd and fiery Arms.
Some natural tears they drop'd, but wip'd them soon;
The World was all before them, where to choose
Their place of rest, and Providence their guide:
They hand in hand with wand'ring steps and slow,
Through Eden took their solitary way.

Nothing could surpass the quality of these lines, but Wordsworth picks up from them and changes their bearing with admirable ease and virtuosity. He is, as it were, returning to a pastoral Eden from exile, leaving behind him the desolate condition brought about by the fall of Adam and Eve. For him, in his time and in his own experience, that condition has come to mean the oppression of the "vast city," from which he has been redeemed. The future prospect, a burdensome challenge in Milton ("The World was all before them, where to choose"), is now a source of buoyancy: "With a heart / Joyous, nor scared at its own liberty, / I look about." Instead of being ushered out of Paradise by "the hast'ning Angel," he is welcomed into it (in its new form) by friendly personifications of nature. The "gentle breeze" is "A visitant that, while he fans my cheek, / Doth seem half-conscious of the joy he brings." And even a "wandering cloud," if he follows it, will turn out to be a "chosen guide" to be trusted: "I cannot miss my way."

Wordsworth also picks up tones from Greek and Latin lyric poetry. Four of the lines just quoted, for instance, sound very much like Propertius and serve as a sudden burst of delighted song amidst the leavened Miltonic effects:

> What dwelling shall receive me? in what vale
> Shall be my harbour? underneath what grove
> Shall I take up my home? and what clear stream
> Shall with its murmur lull me into rest?

The rhythmic pattern of rhapsodic questions is much like Propertius'

> *dicite, quo pariter carmen tenuastis in antro?*
> *quove pede ingressi? quamve bibistis aquam?*

—IV.1

—lines translated in 1917 by Ezra Pound, somewhat freely, as:

> Who hath taught you so subtle a measure,
> in what hall have you heard it;
> What foot beat out your time-bar,
> what water has mellowed your whistles?

—*Homage to Sextus Propertius*

I do not mean to suggest that Wordsworth was deliberately imitating Propertius, or Pound imitating Wordsworth. But there is a broad stream of continuity running through successive generations of artists. Wordsworth's education exposed him to a certain amount of classical verse, as did Pound's. Even more to the point, their own reading did so. The most gifted poets are naturally the ones most open to conscious or unconscious assimilation of what other poets have done—often with just enough of an idiosyncratic turn so that it takes other people's ears time to recognize tonal and rhythmic borrowings and adaptations. There is a huge difference between this necessary continuity and mere inert derivativeness that results from unimaginative imitation. The former, as in Wordsworth's beautifully original use of what he had learned from Milton, partakes of the impersonal process that carries a poem into the phase of magical transport beyond its author's full control. Poetry as an art is so rich in this kind of continuity, which makes all the difference, that one could go on noting and thinking about instances forever, always profitably.

Take, as just one more example, the way that the opening passage of *The Prelude* overlaps with Whitman's writing. Whitman did not use blank verse (although his cadences do often enough approach it); and apart from their shared interest in the common speech, he and Wordsworth seem, on the surface, to have had little in common. Wordsworth died in 1850, five years before *Leaves of Grass* appeared, and Whitman has little to say about him. Nevertheless, as a voracious reader of poetry, he doubtless knew the great British poet's work and seems to have been anticipated by him in certain quite suggestive respects. "With a heart / Joyous, nor scared at its own liberty," Wordsworth writes, "I look about." This phrasing, just a few lines into *The Prelude,* has Whitman's air of nonchalant freedom and self-confidence at the start of *Leaves of Grass* (1855 edition):

> I celebrate myself,
> And what I assume you shall assume,
> For every atom belonging to me as good belongs
>   to you.
>
> I loafe and invite my soul,
> I lean and loafe at my ease . . . . observing a spear
>   of summer grass.

Whitman was more audacious, so that his first readers were even less likely than Wordsworth's to notice his links with poetic predecessors. They of course spotted his departure from conventional metrics, but without giving weight to his adaptation of Biblical cadences. They did not see that, in announcing his theme in his first line (expanded in later editions to "I celebrate myself, and sing myself"), he was following the model for epic poetry established by Homer, Vergil, and Milton. They certainly did not observe that, by putting himself at the center of his epic structure, he was following in Wordsworth's footsteps. Nor were they in position to note that his invention of the form of the poetic sequence was not unrelated to a work like *The Pre-lude,* which Wordsworth arranged as a mosaic of separate experiences, each with its own emotional resonances. Whitman went the long, crucial step farther, eliminating narrative and discursive transitions between the sections in *Song of Myself* and in other sequences and depending on the dynamics of lyrical juxtaposition.

All of which is to say that rapid dismissiveness is not very useful, and that the interested reader (no matter how supposedly learned and clever) should be wary of first impressions. They are necessary and inevitable, and without them we should have no tentative formulations to test against further experience—but they should not become cherished dogma. If a poem has any sort of originality, it will obviously not reveal itself wholly at once to a new reader; as I have suggested, a work of quality reaches a kind of transport that lies beyond even its own author's intentions. Evaluation is a process of empathy that carries us through various stages in repossessing a poem's expressive character: that is, its human relevance and its artistry, in relation both to one another and to the living context of association implicit in its movement. The process is never complete and can never be translated into absolute judgment. Even the most sensitive reader can stumble into one or another of the three dread pitfalls: (1) sentimentality, (2) intransigence, and (3) sheer ignorance:

1) The poems I love may be spinning in my head for the wrong reasons (in the sense of Conrad Aiken's poem that begins: "Music I heard with you was more than music").

2) The poems I shy away from may challenge me in valu-

able ways I am being too obtuse to recognize (in the sense of the notorious review of *The Prelude* that began: "This will never do").

3) The world is full of more poetry than I can possibly discover in my lifetime—poetry that might well alter all my expectations, however flexible (in the sense of Miranda's outcry in *The Tempest:*

O, wonder!
How many goodly creatures are there here!
How beauteous mankind is! O brave new world,
That has such people in't!)

But of one thing I am fairly sure: that it's necessary to live dangerously in these matters and never to abandon direct touch with specific poems when one thinks about poetry. Say what you will about syntactics, semantics, pragmatics, problematics, or the tinkling of phonemes, it will show very little about a poem's particular quality. The only thing one can do, now as in the past, is to connect with what one is reading as responsively as one can at the start, and to go on from there. Opening an anthology of contemporary poetry, for instance, I come upon a poem by Gary Snyder that begins:

The truth
like the belly of a woman turning,
always passes by.
is always true.

"The belly of a woman turning"—slightly sensuous, though not overwhelmingly suggestive. And the redundancy of the note on truth (stressed by the placement of periods) is a problem, although I admit a predilection for sad, dull profundities of this sort. Reading on, however, I see that the first verse-unit may have been a false start, perhaps deliberate. The next two units become more vivid and less obviously sententious: a kind of lament for the common fate of change and suffering and loss, still slightly tinged with the opening coloration:

> throat and tongue—
> do we all feel the same?
> sticky hair curls
>
> quivering throat
> pitch of jaw
> strung pull
> skinnd turn, what will
> be the wrack
> of all the old—

These lines persuade me that "The Truth Like the Belly of a Woman Turning" (despite the banal "do we all feel the same?") is more telling than its first impact suggested, and that perhaps the opening pronouncements (echoed in the banal question for consistency's sake?) are a sort of buffer for the vulnerability of the rest of the poem. But after the astringency of this passage the poem becomes rather forced, ending with effects that shout at us through capitalization, tricks of spelling more extreme than the earlier "skinnd," and the riddling incantatory play of the four closing lines:

> who
> cares.
>   CRYING
> all these passt,
>   losst,
>   years.
>
>   "It always changes"

wind child
wound child

MOTHERS AND DAUGHTERS
live oak and madrone.

I have just rehearsed the usual process of first rapprochement with a poem. Very likely my sense of this poem will remain unsatisfied in some ways, unless for good reason I begin to see it in a new light. Certain questions hang in the air, for the time being at least. Is the poem largely maudlin after all? Is it partly redeemed as a primal, unpretentious expression of one state of feeling—directed toward an older person who has suffered much, perhaps? (Very much *perhaps,* because of the tangle of possibilities suggested by the successive points of attention: at first possibly erotic, then ambiguously suggestive of the pain of the elderly and ill, then alluding to children, and at the end loudly projecting an interesting half-riddle about female generations.) Ranging outside the immediate poem for a moment, one notices its affinities of stylistic eccentricity with the work of two other poets, Robert Duncan and Charles Olson, and more remotely with that of E. E. Cummings. To varied degrees, the poem shares with them tricks of phonetic spelling, distorted syntax, and expressive punctuation: mannerisms sometimes felt within the coteries cultivating them as values in themselves—and outside the coteries, often, as quirks that may or may not work in context.

What is the importance of these affinities for the poem's inner coherence and dynamics? Not very great, I think, except to distract attention from its essential structure and problems. Basically, it is an elegiac poem made up of a series of disparate images, questions, and slightly cryptic aphorisms. It seems half-articulated and half-resolved only. Yet its second and third verse-units point the way toward its becoming a poem of stark, unsentimental loss and lone-liness—toward its reaching a transport of despair, if only the rest of the poem were deleted or drastically altered. It is one of a great many poems that, while far short of being masterpieces or even completely worked through, have their compelling aspects and must be taken seriously.

EPILOGUE

"*Rigor of beauty,*" wrote William Carlos Williams in *Paterson*, "is the quest." Throughout these pages I have stressed the extraordinary freedom—not only in its range of association and reverie, but also in its pursuit of the felt truth of experience—natural to poetry. The poet's full use of this freedom, as Williams implies, depends on a techni-cal mastery that makes every phrase, every effect of rhythm and sound, and every shift in the poem's progression con-tribute tellingly to its dynamic structure.

When this fusion of free imagination and artistic mas-tery occurs, the poet has built better than he or she knew, for the evocative richness of image and idiom is then allowed to draw on memories carried by language through gener-ations. Real poets recognize this magical phase of a poem's emergence out of whatever it sprang from, and cooperate with it wherever it may lead. In a given instance, of course, they may not be able to carry through. I have touched on this question of various gradations of success—from a well-nigh perfect poem like, say, Emily Dickinson's "There's a certain Slant of light" to a brilliant poem like Marvell's "The Picture of Little T.C. in a Prospect of Flowers," which copes powerfully with intractable elements yet may not be a complete triumph; and from Marvell's absorbing effort to John Ashbery's attempt, with indifferent results, to make a further turn on it.[3] The issue of "success," in terms of the definitions offered at the end of Chapter Three—definitions meant to bring out the internal process of poems, rather than to impose a set of criteria not implicit in the process—has little to do with judgmental absolutes. It has to do with bringing to bear all the empathy one can muster, and trying to gauge where the poem has so far arrived. Whatever point the poem has reached, whenever it was "completed," it remains a set of possibilities with, at best, a tentative structure.

Sufficient empathy—and I admit only too readily that here one may, in Gerard Manley Hopkins's phrase, "fable and miss"—allows criticism to be severe without malice. In their conversation and correspondence about each other's poems, poets show this sort of friendly frankness all the time. (Pound's notes on the early drafts of *The Waste Land* are the best-known example.) Thus, in thinking about James Dickey's "Deer among Cattle," I felt a certain loss of focus toward the end: not a judgment that the poem was uninteresting or flat, but simply a perception of overdevelopment beyond its true resolution.[4] By the same token, Mandelstam's poem on Stalin contains self-contradictory or, rather, conflicting tonalities of immense suggestiveness even in translation, so that one largely discounts the somewhat cartoonish diction that might otherwise lead one to consider the piece more polemic than poem.[5] The mag-

[4] See pages 74–69, 45–51, and 54–55 respectively.
[5] See pages 86–90.
[6] See pages 83–86.

netism of its violently painful expression cannot be dis-
missed.

But let me end with a poem, rather than with further
elaboration in prose. The poem, "Erige Cor Tuum ad Me
in Caelum," by H.D. (Hilda Doolittle), acts out the tensions
between hopeful desire for revelation and depressive
awareness of mortality and of an existence empty of meaning. It cannot help sounding triumphant despite itself, for
it implies a transcendence rooted in language and reverie
though not visible outside the human mind. The Latin title
itself, which means "Lift up your heart (or thoughts) to me
in Heaven," is subjected to withering reply but then—very,
very quietly—obeyed in the minimal imagery of the final
verse-unit. All in all, H.D.'s poem speaks directly from the
heart of poetic art and process:

1

Lift up your eyes on high,
under the sky—
indeed?
watch planets swerve and lend
lustre to partner-planet,
as they serve
magnetic stress, and turn
subservient to your hands,
your will that guides
majestic cycle of obedient tides?

lift up our eyes to you?
no, God, we stare and stare,
upon a nearer thing
that greets us here,
Death, violent and near.

2

The alchemy and mystery is this,
no cross to kiss,
but a cross pointing on a compass-face,
east, west, south, north;

the secret of the ages is revealed,
the book un-sealed,
the fisherman entangled in his nets
felled where he waded
for the evening catch,
the house-door
swinging on the broken latch,
the woman with her basket on the quay,
shading her eyes to see,
if the last boat
really is the last,
the house-dog lost,
the little hen escaped,
the precious hay-rick scattered,
and the empty cage,
the book of life is open,
turn and read:

the linnet picking at the wasted seed
is holy ghost,
the weed,
broken by iron axle,
is the flower
magicians bartered for.

Acknowledgments

Georges Borchardt, Inc. John Ashbery: "The Picture of Little J.A. in a Prospect of Flowers." Reprinted by permission of Georges Borchardt, Inc. and the author. Copyright © 1956 by John Ashbery. Faber and Faber Ltd. T. S. Eliot: from "Burnt Norton" Part II. Reprinted by permission of Faber and Faber Ltd. from *Four Quartets* by T. S. Eliot. Philip Larkin: "High Windows" and from "Annus Mirabilis." Reprinted by permission of Faber and Faber Ltd. from *High Windows* by Philip Larkin. Farrar, Straus & Giroux. Elizabeth Bishop: "Five Flights Up" from *The Complete Poems: 1927–1979*, copyright © 1983. Philip Larkin: "High Windows" and lines 1–5 of "Annus Mirabilis" from *High Windows*, copyright © 1974. Robert Lowell: lines 25–48 of "Skunk Hour" from *Selected Poems*, copyright © 1976. Reprinted by permission. Harcourt Brace Jovanovich, Inc. T. S. Eliot: From "Burnt Norton" in *Four Quartets* by T. S. Eliot, copyright 1943 by T. S. Eliot, renewed 1971 by Esme Valerie Eliot. Reprinted by permission of Harcourt Brace Jovanovich, Inc. From "The Boston Evening Transcript" in *Collected Poems 1909–1962* by T. S. Eliot, copyright 1936 by Harcourt Brace Jovanovich, Inc. copyright © 1963, 1964 by T. S. Eliot. Reprinted by permission of the publisher. Harper & Row. Sylvia Plath: "Child" from *The Collected Poems* by Sylvia Plath, copyright © 1981. Reprinted by permission. Harvard University Press. Emily Dickinson: Reprinted by permission of the publishers and the Trustees of Amherst College from *The Poems of Emily Dickinson*, edited by Thomas H. Johnson, Cambridge, Mass. The Belknap Press of Harvard University Press, Copyright 1951, © 1955, 1979, 1983 by the President and Fellows of Harvard College. David Laing. Dilys Laing: "Transience of Pain" by Dilys Laing. Copyright © 1967 by David Laing. Reprinted by permission. New Directions. H. D. (Hilda Doolittle): pages 57–58 of "Erige Cor Tuum ad Me in Caelum" from *Selected Poems* by H. D., copyright © 1957. Ezra Pound: from "Hommage to Sextus Propertius" and "The Coming of War." Ezra Pound, *Personae*. Copyright 1926 by Ezra Pound. From Cantos 83, 4, 76, and 81. Ezra Pound, *The Cantos of Ezra Pound*. Copyright 1934, 1948 by Ezra Pound. Gary Snyder: "The Truth Like the Belly of a Woman Turning." Gary Snyder, *The Back Country*. Copyright © 1966 by Gary Snyder. Reprinted by permission of New Directions Publishing Corporation. Harold Ober Associates. Langston Hughes: "Letter." Reprinted by permission of Harold Ober Associates Incorporated. Copyright 1951 by Langston Hughes. Copyright renewed 1979 by George Houston Bass. Princeton University Press. *Osip Mandelstam's 'Stone'*, trans. Robert Tracy. Copyright © 1981 by Princeton University Press. Excerpt, p. 12, reprinted with permission of Princeton University Press. Random House, Inc. W. H. Auden: "On This Island" from *Collected Poems*, edited by Edward Mendelson. Copyright 1937 and renewed 1965 by W. H. Auden. Reprinted by permission of Random House, Inc. Langston Hughes: "Down and Out" from *Selected Poems of Langston Hughes*. Copyright © 1959 by Langston Hughes. Reprinted by permission of Alfred A. Knopf, Inc. Boris Pasternak: pp. 88–90 of *I Remember: Sketch for an Autobiography*, edited by David Magarshack. Copyright © 1959. Reprinted by permission of Pantheon Books, a Division of Random House, Inc. University of California Press. William Blake: "Introduction" to Songs of Innocence and "Infant Sorrow." From *The Complete Poetry and Prose of William Blake*, edited by David Erdman. Copyright © 1965, 1981 by David V. Erdman. Reprinted by permission of the University of California Press. University of Illinois Press. Michael Harper: "Makin' Jump Shots." From *Images of Kin: New and Selected Poems* by Michael Harper. Copyright © 1977. Reprinted by permission of the author and the University of Illinois Press. A. P. Watt Ltd. W. B. Yeats: from "The Tower," "The People," "Nineteen Hundred and Nineteen," and "The Road at My Door." From *The Poems: A New Edition* by W. B. Yeats. Reprinted by permission of A. P. Watt Ltd., on behalf of Michael B. Yeats and Macmillan London Ltd. Wesleyan University Press. James Dickey: "Deer Among Cattle." Copyright © 1965 by James Dickey. Reprinted from *Poems 1956–1967* by permission of Wesleyan University Press. This poem first appeared in *Shenandoah, Summer*.

Certain passages, in their original form, have appeared or are scheduled to appear in *Approaches to Teaching T. S. Eliot, Catalan Review, EIDOS, New York Times Book Review, Paideuma, Southern Review*, and *Yeats: An Annual of Critical and Textual Studies*. The author's translations of poems by J. V. Foix and Rainer Maria Rilke appeared originally in *Translation* and *Poetry Review*.

Index